KV-571-337

1000024816

International Landscape Design

International Landscape Design

Robert Holden

Co-ordinating researcher Jennifer Hudson

 Laurence King

712 HOL

Published 1996 by Laurence King Publishing
an imprint of Calmann & King Ltd
71 Great Russell Street
London WC1B 3BN

Copyright © 1996 Calmann & King Ltd

All rights reserved. No part of this publication may
be reproduced or transmitted in any form or by
any means, electronic or mechanical, including
photocopy, recording or any information storage
and retrieval system, without permission in writing
from the publisher.

A catalogue record for this book is available from
the British Library.

ISBN 1 85669 085 7

Designed by Nicole Griffin

Printed in Hong Kong

The author would like to thank Jo Lightfoot and Jennifer Hudson at
Laurence King for their guidance, help and patience; all the designers
who sent in valuable material and so made this book possible; and
Helen, William and Elisabeth for their support and tolerance.

Contents

This book is a review of the progress of landscape design worldwide in the 1990s. Any such review is of its nature selective. As a general guideline work must have been completed in the 1990s, though some projects which are long term were begun in the 1980s, for example the Zoetermeer Floriade. One of the points of interest of a Dutch Floriade or garden festival is that it is planned and executed over a decade and, rather like the Bundesgartenschauen in Germany, it aims to achieve an effect of 20- or 30-year maturity for the festival opening.

Two other projects break the 1990s guideline. One is Hafeninsel Park in Saarbrücken by Latz + Partner, which is of seminal importance as a post-industrial project from the late 1980s and is necessary for an understanding of the background to Latz's later Duisburg Nord Park. The other project from the 1980s is Robert Camlin's Uppermill Cemetery in Saddleworth, England.

White River State Park in Indianapolis is an interesting exception to the general rule that projects must have been carried out and built or planted: it was a proposal, a design study and planning advocacy exercise involving an existing grain mill and silos, and therefore the potential of the project is physically demonstrable. This project is included because it may prove an object lesson, applicable elsewhere, in appreciation of an industrial landscape.

The most recent projects illustrated were completed in mid-1995, and some schemes (such as Duisburg Nord Park or John Lyle's Center for Regenerative Studies) will continue to be developed into the next century; indeed the interest of the Center for Regenerative Studies is as a changing, living, educational and research community. Landscape design can involve planning advocacy, and as a design discipline it is particularly involved with long-term change; it is seldom fixed and static.

Private gardens and historic landscape park and garden conservation schemes have been excluded. Bryant Park, New York, is the closest to a historic urban park conserved, but it is included because Laurie Olin has reworked a 1930s Beaux Arts design in an avowed continuation of that tradition. Landscape architecture, like the fine arts, can involve *hommage* and reworkings.

The majority of the projects are the work of landscape architects. This book is not narrowly professional in its view, however, because the art of landscape design crosses many disciplines and, though landscape architecture can be a focus, the work of architects, environmentalists and environmental artists is often equally valid. It is also noteworthy that Spain is a country where the profession of landscape architecture is only just beginning, and much of the incredible expansion of public parks and garden and urban space provision in Spain that dates from the early 1980s has been designed by architects.

As the projects have been chosen for their physical design interest, much of the non-design work of landscape architects has not been illustrated. There are no environmental impact assessments or large-scale planning studies – though the Emscher Park can be considered a form of regional planning through practical ecological development and design which can lead to large-scale economic benefits. This book is devoted to the opposite of paper design; it deals with projects that have been created by the process Lancelot Brown described as "place-making". Sometimes that process involves strong individual designs which are like patterns on the ground: for example, some aspects of the work of Peter Walker or Martha Schwartz. Sometimes the process is one achieved essentially on site by subtly fitting new development into an existing habitat. That way of working is most obvious in the eco-tourism schemes such as EcoSystems' work at Seven Spirit Wilderness in Arnhem Land on the tip of northern Australia. It is obvious on a larger scale in the tourist resort at Langkawi Beach, Malaysia, by the Kuala Lumpur office of Aspinwall Clouston, or on a more subtle scale in the work of the Environmental Design Partnership at the Taung Monument on the edge of the Kalahari Desert. Both Seven Spirit Wilderness and the Taung Monument are schemes designed to promote employment and economic benefits. In other projects one can see a collaborative, choreographic approach, such as John Lyle's work with his student community at the Center for Regenerative Studies in Los Angeles, where not only the application but also the inspiration came from student work.

The aim of this book is to give a worldwide view of landscape architecture which otherwise could only be achieved by means of reading many, sometimes obscure, periodicals and magazines supplemented by widespread visits. Some of the projects are previously

Moscow's Detski Park/Children's Park proposal was the subject of a design competition in 1990-1 won by the late Alexei Meshcherjakov and Oleg Tolkatchev, both from Professor Kvasov's landscape course at the Moscow Architecture Institute. The design is a rich and ikon-like piece which illustrates the interest in reinterpreting historicism in the Moscow School.

8

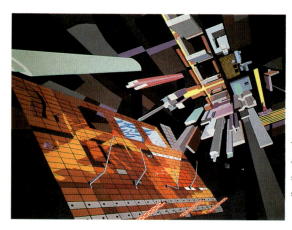

The Schouwburgplein in central Rotterdam is a strongly articulated urban space in metal and light.

Jamie Liversedge's design for a new college campus for the Stichting Voor Gelderse Hogescholen in Arnhem, The Netherlands, is remarkable for its strong colours and pattern. Through the centre of the plaza runs a lowered bicycle park canyon for 1,400 bicycles.

unpublished. It is an impression rather than an exhaustive survey; we do not make a claim for absolute completeness of coverage – sometimes it is extraordinarily difficult to persuade that often humblest and most unassuming of professionals, the landscape architect, to allow his or her work to be broadcast. The key criterion for inclusion was whether a scheme was seen as interesting and arresting.

It is particularly pleasing to include the work of Robert Camlin who has been little published and is one of the most gifted of English landscape architects. Uppermill Cemetery has not been published before (except in a regional professional newsletter) and this project marks the beginning of a new development in British landscape design: the interest in and use of vernacular and regional materials such as the stone and drystone walls of the Pennines at Saddleworth. Something of this was later seen in 1992 at the Ebbw Vale Garden Festival in the work of Eachus Huckson and in Will Williams' Wave Wall. This interest has been further stimulated by the works of environmental artists such as Andrew Goldsworthy.

The book is divided into five sections: post-industrial; parks and recreation; ecology and conservation; urban design and housing; and offices and institutions. The categories are not mutually exclusive: a post-industrial landfill scheme like Byxbee Landfill or the conserved steelworks at Duisburg Nord are also public parks. However, the categories do allow interesting groupings which reveal some of the developments of landscape design thinking as we approach the end of the millennium.

One of these developments is a concern about the future of the nineteenth- and twentieth-century city as old industries and commercial areas go out of use. Schemes such as the Parc del Litoral in Barcelona by Martorell Bohigas Mackay show a way of rejuvenating old dock areas by means of open space development and a way of handling new urban road and transport systems in a form of large-scale redevelopment. At The Citadel in Los Angeles Martha Schwartz has created a sense of place in a retail and commercial development using the shell of an old tyre factory. Throughout Europe and North America new city squares and plazas have been created or old ones remade in order to rejuvenate rundown commercial areas (for example, Bryant Park, New York, or Pershing Square, Los Angeles), while elsewhere forms of urban design are seen as central to new suburban or settlement design (for example, Parc de Catalunya in Sabadell, Barcelona, or Joondalup Park in Western Australia).

Joondalup Park is also an illustration of another theme of contemporary landscape design: that of using natural or wild plant communities and other wildlife to form the basis for strong design, and using design to interplay with natural process. In Western Australia the natural savannah requires a frugal approach to the use of water and is in itself intolerant of dense human use; therefore the challenge is how to work with such a landscape and how to accommodate new development without fundamental damage. At the other end of the development process is the work of George Hargreaves in the United States. He is creating areas of natural process on old landfill sites, areas where there are varieties of exposure, shelter, wetness and dryness and where the geomorphology of the landscape is in a dialogue with ecological process in a way that has a poetic meaning. John Lyle and his students at Caltech are also working on a landfill site, and the community that is the Center for Regenerative Studies is a laboratory of ideas for how to regenerate and reuse and take care of land. Landscape design can be didactic and experimental. Land, which *is* landscape as seen and valued by man, is a finite resource, and as the developed world and developing countries become more and more urbanized, it is increasingly necessary to think about ways of recycling land and giving it a value.

Other contemporary themes include geometry as repetition for emphasis, as in the work of Peter Walker at Plaza Tower, Orange County, California, where he literally reflected the tower façade by Cesar Pelli in the plaza design. Geometry can also be used as Adriaan Geuze of West 8 uses it in The Netherlands, that most linear and geometric of countries, where his Shell Project on the Oosterschelde barrage is a series of black and white lines, but lines that will be subject to change and the disappearance caused by weathering and sand burial.

Sometimes landscape architects work in a poetic and allegorical way, as does George Hargeaves, or indeed Shunmyo Masuno at the National Metallurgical Institute plaza, which tells the story of mineral prospecting. Sometimes poets and artists work jointly with landscape architects, and there are two

prime examples of that process in this book. At Grevenbroich Schlosspark, Professor Ian Hamilton Finlay, the Scottish artist and poet, has worked with landscape architect Georg Penker to produce a place full of literary reference and conceit in a way, typical of Hamilton Finlay, that causes one to think; words have meaning and landscape can have meanings too. The Kinnear sisters, Lynn and Susan, are landscape architect and painter, respectively. At Hellings Street Play Area, Lynn Kinnear took a painting by her sister and used it as an inspiration for both composition and colour. At Louisiana Lake Garden, Lea Nørgaard and Vibeke Holscher worked with the Italian sculptor Alfio Bonanno to produce a landscape where the play sculpture almost literally grows out of the place.

There are some strong design schools of landscape architects: Harvard, Versailles and the Amsterdam Academie van Bouwkunst seem to be especially influential at present. Harvard is the school of Peter Walker and Martha Schwartz, but currently also has the Englishman James Corner teaching there. Versailles (the Ecole Nationale Supérieure du Paysage) is the school that has produced the majority of the members of the small but very strong, design-led landscape architecture profession in France, and indeed was the only recognized school in the country until the 1980s. This book features the work of Gustafson (an American educated at Versailles) and Vexlard, but it is also necessary to mention the work of Christophe Girot who is director at Versailles. In Holland Adriaan Geuze teaches at the Amsterdam School and is beginning to have an enormous influence on other landscape architects. His scheme for the Schouwburgplein in Rotterdam is nearing completion as this book goes to press.

Schemes to look forward to for the future include London-based Jamie Liversedge's work on a major educational plaza in Arnhem, The Netherlands. There is also much promise in the former command economies of Eastern Europe and Russia, for example the work of former students from the Moscow Architecture Institute landscape course. One example given here from the very end of Soviet times, the Detski Park proposal in Moscow, shows something of the great promise of landscape architecture worldwide.

Bürgerpark auf der Hafeninsel, Saarbrücken, Germany (see page 23). The *Wassertor* (watertower) seen from the naturally regenerated area to the east. Beyond it is the viaduct of the access road to the A620 Autobahn.

1 Post-Industrial

Duisburg Nord Landscape Park

Duisburg, Germany

Latz + Partner

The 200-hectare Duisburg Nord Landscape Park is a project of huge ambition, physically and aesthetically. The aesthetic ambition calls for a revolution in one's thinking of what a park can be. Almost by simple semantics a huge steelworks has been translated into a park in which former steelworkers' families climb to the top of blast furnaces, 50 or 60 metres high, below which grows an ecological park based on natural regeneration. Heavy metal bands sing out from heaps of slag, and mountaineering clubs scale the mass concrete structure of former industry.

The old A.G. Thyssen steelworks, just north of Duisburg, closed in 1985. In 1989 it was decided that the area should be made into a city park as a joint project by the City of Duisburg and the Emscher Park IBA (see page 19). Then followed an international design competition that was won by Professor Peter Latz and Anna-Liese Latz. The 200-hectare steelworks is to be part of the overall IBA project for 300 square kilometres of green space in this part of the Ruhrgebiet. The Duisburg Nord Landscape Park is a long-term project that will go on into the next century at a cost of £28 million, but it was sufficiently advanced to be formally opened to the public in 1994.

The design is based on an appreciation of the industrial inheritance: lines of old railway embankment are seen as a form of land art and will be managed as grassland. Visitors can wander through the site and from the embankments view the land around with a sense of liberation. Formerly this part of Duisburg was very claustrophobic and the public were restricted to the low areas beyond the walls and below the embankments. The structures of the steelworks are being conserved in a way that makes them safe enough to climb, but also allows them to rust.

The project is colour coded: red represents the earth; grey and rusting areas are *verboten*, areas that cannot be entered or climbed; while blue means areas that are open and can be touched.

There are two fundamental ecological principles guiding the development of the park. Firstly, the recycling of materials on the site both as a medium for plant growth and as building material; for example, bricks are ground up to make the aggregate for red concrete. This idea of recycling is one that the Latzes had already used at Hafeninsel Park in Saarbrücken (see page 23). There are demonstration gardens in the coke and ore bunkers which use coal, ore and metal as growing mediums.

The second ecological idea is that of the water cycle. The park is crossed by a polluted waste water channel called the Old Emscher and it is necessary to clean this water. Surface water from the roofs, roads and paved areas is directed by open drainage channels into cooling basins and old settling tanks. The water has to be purified of dust contaminants and this is done by a wind-powered water drop on the site of the old sintering plant. The water is passed into the Old Emscher where there will be different water zones from vegetated bank areas with a depth of 10-50 centimetres, settlement areas up to 2.5 metres deep and gravel and sand banks.

Great iron plates found in the casting area for pig iron have been composed to make a square, the Piazza Metallica, consisting of 47 panels, each 2.5 metres square and weighing 7.5-8.5 tonnes, laid on sand. The plates were cleaned by compressed air and high-pressure hose to reveal a surface that makes the frozen molten steel appear like ice. Meanwhile, by the south-eastern entrance an urban farm has been established.

In totality, this park is a new way of liberating the history of the working man and of making the inheritance of industry the basis of something new rather than destroying it or hiding it away.

Opposite:
A bunker garden interior. Hydrangea, fern and moss gardens are being established in the coke and ore bunkers. Plants came from abroad with the iron ore from Norway, Brazil, South Africa and Australia and have naturalized on the ash, slag and other materials. In total there are 240 plant species existing on the site, most of them immigrants.

The railway walkway is a reconstruction of a former overhead railway, which allows people to walk across the bunkers and look down into gardens and water basins. The rails have still to be re-layed in this photograph and ultimately there will be rail-mounted mobile facilities.

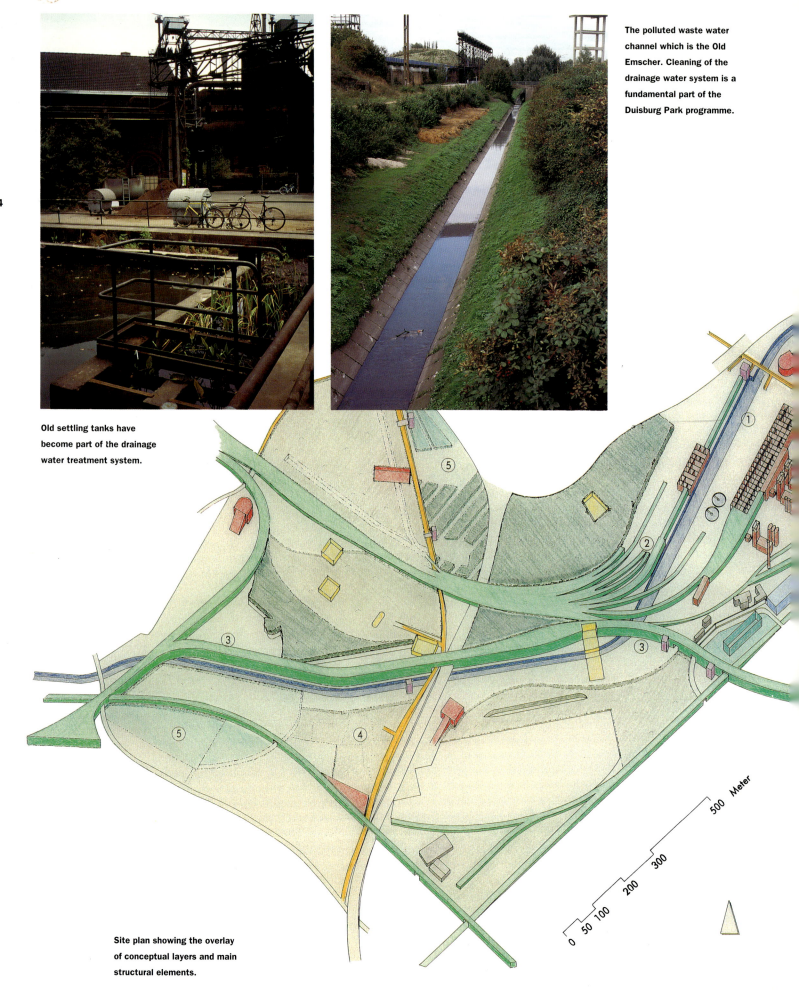

The polluted waste water channel which is the Old Emscher. Cleaning of the drainage water system is a fundamental part of the Duisburg Park programme.

Old settling tanks have become part of the drainage water treatment system.

Site plan showing the overlay of conceptual layers and main structural elements.

500 Meter

0 50 100 200 300

Above: Old mass concrete walls become training grounds for local mountaineering clubs.

Water park:

1 Canal

Parks and walks on old railway lines:

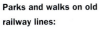

2 Railway sidings

3 Embankment walks

Varieties of vegetation:

low vegetation

bushes

thick woodland

symbolic gardens

existing parks

4 allotments **5** sports areas

look-out gardens

landmark feature gardens

industrial museum

cultural buildings

trade buildings

walkway

16

The blast furnaces are seen as observation towers or "Matterhorns" which visitors can climb and mount.

The view down into the bunker gardens.

The metal skeleton of old industry is being naturalized and made green.

Emscher Landscape Park

River Emscher Valley, Rheinland-Westfalen, Germany

IBA Emscher Park

The Emscher Park Internationale Bauausstellung (IBA) is a ten-year programme of environmental improvements in the tradition of international exhibitions and the West Berlin IBA of the 1980s. The Emscher Park IBA was set up in 1989 by the Länder government of Nordrhein-Westfalen to operate until 1999.

The River Emscher catchment runs from Duisburg on the Rhine east to Dortmund and is an area where heavy industry is in decline. The main industries, such as coal and steel mining, began to close down in the 1960s. The regional government was concerned that there should be effective action within ten years. It saw an area suffering economic, social and environmental problems and found a way forward which put the environment and ecology of the region first. Every project has to show a net ecological gain.

The IBA has the following main aims:

- the ecological regeneration of the 350-kilometre length of the River Emscher and its tributaries
- the creation of the Emscher Landscape Park (300 square kilometres of parks and green spaces linked by paths and cycle routes)
- the upgrading of 3,000 existing homes and the building of 3,000 new homes
- job-creation schemes based on a chain of 22 technology centres set in new parkland
- new uses for industrial buildings and landmarks.

The IBA is government-led. Two-thirds of the total programme of DM 2.5 billion comes from Federal and Länder government or European Union funding, and one-third from the private sector. So far, the IBA has sponsored some 92 projects.

The boldest is the reclamation of the River Emscher, which, in the nineteenth century, was sacrificed to carrying industrial waste and domestic sewage. Floods led to typhoid epidemics, so in 1904 the Emschergenossenschaft was set up by the municipalities and industrial concerns to stop flooding by building dikes and lining the river and its tributaries with concrete. The decline of mining (and the ending of land subsidence) allows the removal of the concrete, and the cleaning of the river allows the removal of the dikes and the naturalization of the 350-kilometre river system.

Continuing industrial pollution will now be led into a piped system to five new sewage treatment

Opposite: The Erin coal mine in Castrop-Rauxel is one of the many mines and coal tips to be rescued, vegetated and developed as part of the Emscher Park's ten-year programme of ecologically-led regional development.

19

Wissenschaftspark Rheinelbe (science park) in Gelsenkirchen, opened in 1995 on the site of a former steelworks and a mere ten minutes' walk from the mainline railway station.

plants. Once pollution is dealt with, the early twentieth-century dikes along the River Emscher itself will be removed and the water meadows allowed to flood. This is a long-term programme which will take 20 to 30 years.

Linked to the regeneration of the river is the creation of the 300-square-kilometre Emscher Landscape Park, which will be a green lung for the cities and their two million inhabitants. The idea in the Ruhr is to create easily accessible parkland and green spaces within the conurbation, linked by footpath and cycle routes. One such project is the Duisburg Nord Park (see page 13); another is the 1997 Gelsenkirchen Bundesgartenschau or Garden Festival on the site of the old Nordsten mine to a landscape masterplan by Wilheim Dreschhoff, Christina Plassmann and Thomas Wilken. Some 270 kilometres of cycle routes and 130 kilometres of footpaths have been established.

There are also new housing and the refurbishment of old like the pithead village of Sohüngelberg built in 1906 in the English garden suburb style to serve the Hugo coal mine. New employment is provided in developments such as the Wissenschaftspark Rheinelbe (science park) on the site of an old steelworks and colliery near the centre of Gelsenkirchen. On a larger scale is the Gewerbepark Erin (business park) in Castrop-Rauxel set in a landscape park designed by Professor Pridik.

This is a very significant exercise in sub-regional regeneration based on placing environmental and ecological concerns first, but linked to employment, housing and economic regeneration. The programme is an important example for other industrialized landscapes of the world.

Gewerbepark Erin (business park) in Castrop-Rauxel, a 40-hectare site, on the site of the former Erin coal mine and adjacent to the town centre. It is based on a comprehensive landscape plan. The Erin coal mine was developed by an Irishman.

A concrete-lined tributary of
the River Emscher.

Typical view after the removal
of a concrete channel and
restoration of a natural
watercourse, here the
Deininghauser Bach (brook),
east of Castrop-Rauxel.

Another view of the restored
Deininghauser Bach.

Bürgerpark auf der Hafeninsel

Saarbrücken, Saarland, Germany

Latz + Partner

The site for this park was the old coaling docks on the River Saar, which were heavily bombed in the Second World War and had remained as wasteland ever since. The island, the Hafeninsel (Harbour island), was covered with rubble and the docks lay ruinous. On the sourthern bank facing the island is the A620 Autobahn, which effectively has made that stretch of the river a straight concrete channel.

Latz + Partner wished to use the site, its history and traces of the past and the ruined monuments of industry. The scheme began in 1979 and was a precursor to the Duisburg Nord Park (see page 13). As they were to do later in Duisburg, the Latzes began the design by defining layers. The first layer was to create or reinstate a network of urban roads so that the park and the town were connected. The northern channel around the island was filled in to make connections across it easy, and they followed the grid of the old Prussian Ordnance Survey maps in order to recall that nineteenth-century aspect of the town's history. The second layer was the chain of new public gardens cut from the hills of rubble; these open spaces also link town and park and help make the Hafeninsel open (formerly, as a dock, it was closed to public access). The third layer was based on the preservation of existing traces of the site, including paving and the naturally regenerated vegetation (such as chicory, thistles, sorrel and alder). The fourth layer involved the monuments of industry such as buildings, coal bunkers, the overhead railway and even the old barges moored in the River Saar.

There are three significant new garden areas. The Garden of Rest (Ruhegarten) was made by excavating into a hill of bomb rubble in order to create in a quiet enclosure a paradise garden of fruit trees, flowers and water-play, and an open-air theatre. There is also the triangular field and Italian Valley where, on 400-square-metre plots, local citizens have made community gardens with rocks and stones gathered from the site. Under the bridge that crosses the site and leads over the River Saar to the Autobahn junction is a collecting point for all the surface water drainage on the site. This is raised in a water wall and falls in order to refresh and oxygenate the water.

Behind this scheme was a whole series of local endeavours of youth and community participation and training to create a new park outside the usual German system of Federal and local Ländesgartenschauen.

Opposite: The theatre and gardens in the Garden of Rest (Ruhegarten), created by excavating into a hill of bomb rubble.

Right: The triangular field with communal plots made by local residents using materials from the site.

The line of paths picked out by old rubble walls with naturally regenerated vegetation around.

24

**New seats have been inserted
into the rubble walls.**

Rubble walls made from local
materials.

Workers recover old sett
paving.

26

Natural regeneration on old bunkers and the overhead railway.

The bricklined pool and islet in the Garden of Rest.

The *Wassertor* (watertower) where surface water drainage from the site is collected and cascaded in order to oxygenate it.

28

Key

1 Benches along levee with waste receptacles

2 Shell band: 15cm wide

3 Flare

4 Keyhole

5 Decks

6 Existing vegetation on levee remains

7 Hillocks planted with lupins

8 Arc berms

9 Wind wave piece

10 Hedgerow

11 Weirs

12 Phase I limit of fill and planting

13 Gravel road

14 1.5m separation

15 Asphalt dike/pedestrian path

16 Eucalyptus trees

17 Gravel parking with concrete kerb

18 Restrooms

19 Oyster shell path

20 Chevrons

21 Benches along perimeter path

22 Existing *Baccharis piluaris consanguinea* expanded

23 Landgate

24 Weirs

25 Directional signs at path intersections

26 Pole field

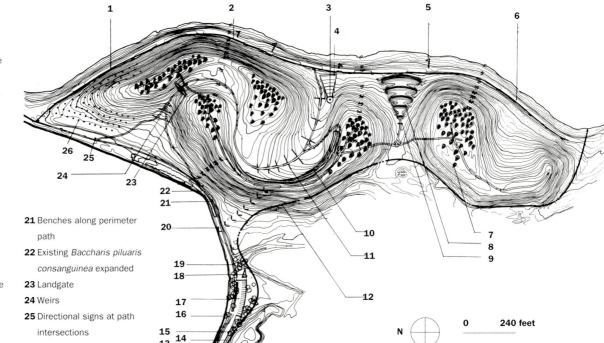

N

0   240 feet

Byxbee Landfill Park in San Francisco Bay. These are completely new landforms made of landfill basically two v-shaped hills patterned in various ways.

The small mounds of earth covered with fresh green growth. The mounds lie on top of the hillocks of landfill and recall the mounds of shells left in the area by the Ohlone Indians. Across the bay are the hangars of Palo Alto airstrip.

The field of poles at the northern end of the park; the top of each pole forms a level plane below which the grassland undulates.

1.4

Byxbee Landfill Park

Palo Alto, California, USA

Hargreaves Associates

Byxbee Park lies on 12 hectares of landfill up to 18 metres high on the edge of San Francisco Bay and set between the tidal marshes of the bay, Palo Alto Airport and a remaining working area of landfill. The rubbish tips have been capped with clay and 30 centimetres of topsoil and reshaped. The design influences include the technical requirements of landfill sites, the situation and its views of sea and marsh, and its coastal exposure. Surrounding the site is a plethora of man-made objects from electricity pylons to radio masts. This is a place at which to watch birds and planes.

Land reclamation of the landfill has dictated the forms and vegetation of the park: no trees could be planted because their roots would penetrate the clay capping layer, so it is a design of landform, systems of controlling erosion on the hillsides, and native grasses. Methane from the rotting rubbish has to be tapped and burned, and there is a methane gas flare in the centre of the park, invisible in daytime except for the shadow of the flame seen in a bed of white gravel that forms a keyhole shape.

Small mounds are arranged in large groups on top of the hillocks of rubbish fill. These provide wind shelter and elevation for people to sit and view the bay. They are inspired by the mounds of shells left by the Ohlone Indians in prehistory. The mounds are aligned against prevailing winds. Below the hillocks, arc berms control erosion. Footpaths of oyster shells pass weirs, and on the central ridge line is a hedgerow of Myoporum (*Myoporum laetum*), Broom Teatree (*Leptospermum scoparium*) and Manzanita (*Arcostaphyllos franciscana*). A 15-centimetre band of oyster shells also marks the top of the levee along the eastern shore of the park.

The line of Palo Alto airstrip is continued through the park in the form of precast road barriers arranged as chevrons to form the ground-to-air signal "Do not land yet". The concrete barriers slow rainwater run-off and create moist habitats for wild flowers. A forest of telegraph poles covers the north-eastern slopes and their tops are cut to form a horizontal plane while the ground rises and falls beneath.

The whole park is clothed with short native grasses dominated by Needlegrass (*Stipa pulchra*), which gives a bright emerald green in spring and golden colours in the summer, in contrast to the green of the marsh grass in the bay. Escort Wheatgrass (*Agropyron sp.*) has also been planted to aid sward establishment and this will die out in two to three years. It is interesting that much of this park's approach to dealing with change and form, and some of the techniques, such as the use of oyster shells, are shared with Adriaan Geuze's Shell Project in The Netherlands (see page 93) and that at first viewing the results appear so utterly different.

Precast concrete blocks form chevrons and pick up the line of Palo Alto airstrip. From the air the chevrons read as the signal "Do not land yet".

30

The medieval village recalls the days when Alsace was part of the Hapsburgs' Holy Roman Empire. This view from the château tower is of the medieval layout with the forest beyond.

The old potash mine buildings are to become an industrial museum.

1.5

Ecomusée d'Alsace

Ungersheim, Alsace, France

EDAW Jarvis France

In the 1970s a group of students came up with the idea of creating a medieval village. Eventually a site was found at an old potash mine just north of Pulversheim between Mulhouse and Guebwiler in Alsace. In 1990 EDAW was asked to develop a masterplan for a major expansion of the village, integrating the abandoned potash mine buildings and spoil heaps within a total site area of 90 hectares.

The principal objectives were to make an overall masterplan. This included the creation of links and transport infrastructure, with a tramway, a canal and boats on the 10-hectare lake; the stabilization of the steep slopes of the potash heaps; the reorganization of car-parking within the Rhine forest, and the creation of development zones adjacent to the village such as holiday villages and hotels. The masterplan covered the medieval village with its related theme gardens such as a physic garden, vineyard, kitchen gardens, the parterre garden of the château and farmyard areas; it also included a romantic garden linking the medieval village to the canal, and an eighteenth-century street. Gravel extraction has led to the phased creation of a lake, and clay and topsoil from the gravel pit were used for the stabilization of the potash spoil heaps.

View of farm buildings and kitchen garden close to the château. Such views make it difficult to recall that this was formerly an area of potash mining.

This was an extremely polluted site due to a history of 200 years of potash extraction. There was also the challenge of limited funds, the matter of recycling material and the conflict between the theme of the medieval village and the fact of a nineteenth-century industrial environment. Timescale and budget were not defined and much of the volunteer labour was inexperienced and unskilled.

The site is accessible from the D430 road to the west and is bordered on the west by the old potash mine and its spoil heap. From the mine buildings runs a tramway circuit. Visitors who come by car are accommodated in one big car-park set into forest and served by the tramway. The routes from the car-park are either an undulating line, which becomes the road through the medieval village and leads on to the new lake, or a straight axis leading to the potash mine works, which are to become an industrial museum.

The potash mine lies to the south (bottom), and on the east (right) is the River Thur. The car-parks are sited to the east.

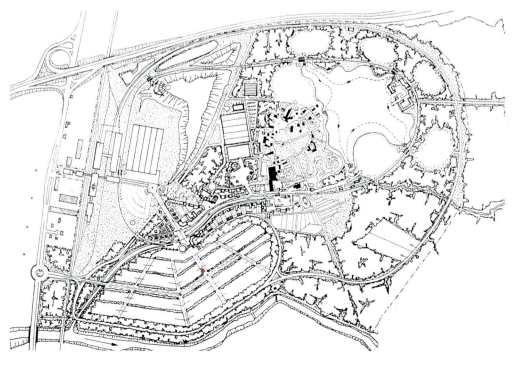

1.6
The Lakeside Gardens

Ebbw Vale Garden Festival/Gwyl Gerddi Cymru Ebbw Vale 1992, Wales, UK

Eachus Huckson Landscape Architects

The Welsh National Garden Festival in 1992 was the last of the biennial series which began in Britain with the Liverpool International Garden Festival in 1984. At Ebbw Vale an 80-hectare site was developed on heavily polluted land that formerly had been a coal mine and old steelworks at the head of the valley of the River Ebbw.

Old slag heaps were retained and water diverted to cascade down into the new lake designed by Eachus Huckson. This new lake was at the end of the main Garden Festival axis, approached through a line of semi-mature *Metasequioa glyptostroboides* which led to the red Torii arch, by sculptor Richard Darke, and which introduced the lake itself. At the far side there was a Japanese pavilion (both arch and pavilion were obeisances to the Japanese investment in South Wales).

The lake, which is in three sections, was designed to create a series of changing views as visitors walked around it. The northern part of the lake by

The Torii arch by Richard Darke, with the Japanese pavilion beyond.

the Torii arch has crisp concrete edges, and around the arch the pavement is in granite setts and local slate. The southern pool has south-facing lawns, timber decks and a sand beach. Between the two areas runs a channel which is simply edged in wood, and this was intended to provide a setting for a proposed Japanese garden.

The Japanese pavilion is set on a promontory on the main north-south axis and given a woodland mound as a backdrop. The Lakeside Gardens are representative of the achievement at Ebbw Vale, which was the most strongly masterplanned and best designed of the British Garden Festivals and where much of the open space was designed for long-term use. British landscape architects learned a great deal from the experience of the Festivals and it is lamentable that the programme has come to an end: they were one of the few examples in the 1980s in Britain of investment in parks and urban open space as a way of revitalizing declining industrial areas.

View across the new lake, set in the valley bottom of Ebbw Vale and dominated by an industrial slagheap that was retained.

Opposite: Superb detailing of stone, setts and pebbles by the northern pool.

Looking across the Palm Court
with its 250 date palms and
chequerboard of grey and red
concrete paviors.

1.7
The Citadel

City of Commerce, California, USA

Martha Schwartz/Ken Smith/David Meyer

The Uniroyal Tire and Rubber Plant fronting Santa Ana Freeway was designed in 1929 as an Assyrian temple to the tyre. Redeveloped and renamed "The Citadel", the freeway frontage has been retained while the remainder of the site has been rebuilt as offices, a shopping mall, a hotel and, of course, a car-park.

The tyre factory closed in 1978, and in 1986 Texas developer Trammell Crow Company with architects The Nadel Partnership won the City of Commerce competition for the site on the basis of keeping the front of the tyre factory. Landscape architect Martha Schwartz's response to the brief was to cut a 50-metre swath out of the half-kilometre long freeway frontage to make way for automobile access and give freeway users a glimpse of what lay beyond. She then created a car-park plaza on the parade: 250 date palms (*Phoenix dactylifera*) lined up on a chequerboard pattern of grey and red concrete paviors, with a white precast concrete "tyre" round each tree. She thus subsumes the conventional road engineering vocabulary of the parking lot into a design of pattern, line and perspective with meanings that refer to the history of the site: the car is put in its place.

The palm court separates the shops and office buildings and carves out a civic space from the urban freeway fringe which is Los Angeles. There are references here to Assyria (an oasis of date palms), to the car culture of Los Angeles and to southern California's agricultural groves. This design shows how urban memories can be retained by creative conservation and how a coherence can be created out of commerce and the automobile on a low-cost budget.

Left: The lines of the Palm Court, which separates shops and office buildings, looking across to the Santa Ana freeway and the back of the Uniroyal factory building.

Below: White, precast concrete "tyres", red and light and dark grey concrete blocks set in a simple pattern and offset by the blocks of grass and groundcover.

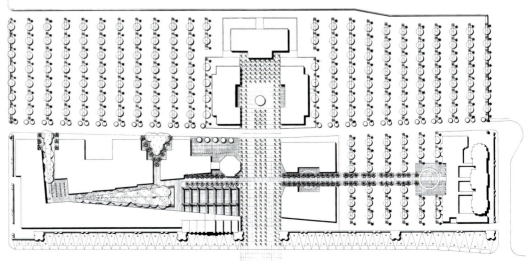

The plan: an exercise in formal geometry to create new urban spaces and orchestrate the impact of car-parks.

The mills set in proposed
meadowland.

The mills, meadowland and a new
woodland and canal axis.

The silos seen in relation to
downtown Indianapolis.

White River State Park Proposal

Indianapolis, Indiana, USA

Eric Fulford at Rundell Ernstberger Associates

The Acme Evans mills and grain silos were built between 1918 and 1936 on the east bank of the White River, and the 27 silos dominated the skyline of downtown Indianapolis. Such Midwestern silos inspired Le Corbusier in his *Vers une Architecture* of 1923 and they were a characteristic landmark of the twentieth-century Midwestern landscape. This book is devoted to landscape architecture as achieved, and so almost invariably the projects are those that have been achieved, built and planted. This is the sort of project that tests that rule, because the silos were demolished in July 1994 by the White River State Park Commission despite the landscape architects' recommendations: the landmarks had been built; it is the vision that failed.

The State Park Commission was set up in the 1970s to celebrate Indiana's past by creating a park on both sides of the White River. In fact relatively little of the proposed parkland has been made. In 1988 the Commission bought the mills in order to demolish them and build an Omni Imax theatre. It proposed to save and conserve only the superintendent's building from the mill complex.

Eric Fulford's scheme involved reusing the grain mill and its silos for a relocated Indiana State Museum. This would have linked with the existing nearby Eiteljorg Museum of American Indian and Western Art. Basic to Fulford's proposals was the idea of locating buildings to the edge of the site so a new park could have been created between Washington Street and the river.

This park design was based on an overlay of the regular geometry of promenades and open views through woodland, and a natural or irregular geometry of meandering canal through riverside meadows allowed to flood periodically. The proposals aimed to capture the identity of the particular place by representing the native landscape and the processes of river erosion and deposition to symbolize the once vast ancient forests, agriculture and industry of Indiana.

This is a record of what was and what could have been if people's eyes and sensibilities had been open to the appreciation of their inheritance.

Right: The grain silos in their original state, photographed by Marsh Davis.

Below: The end of the mills in mid-1994.

Eric Fulford's overall site plan.

Louisiana Lake Garden,
Humlebaek, Denmark (see
page 41). The "opera house"
visible through the branches
of a weeping willow (*Salix
babylonica*).

2 Parks & Recreation

The "opera house" made from the prow of a boat by Anders Thygesen dates from 1978 and is seen framed through Alfio Bonanno's bridge. This scene gives a good idea of the wilderness feel that Lea Nørgaard and Vibeke Holscher have successfully retained.

2.1

Louisiana Lake Garden

Humlebaek, Denmark

Lea Nørgaard & Vibeke Holscher

The Lake Garden is set in the park of the Louisiana Museum of Art. It lies beside the Humlebaek Lake, which was enlarged and connected to the sea during the Napoleonic Wars to provide a haven for warships. In the nineteenth century the fortifications fell into disuse and the harbour became a woodland lake.

In 1978 the lakeside was briefly opened to the public, but it was closed in 1980 and the area was neglected and became wild. The first stage of the new lakeside garden was opened in 1994 in connection with the new Children's House at Louisiana. The museum has always had a policy of welcoming children and the building of the special house and surrounding landscape is an extension of that policy.

Lea Nørgaard and Vibeke Holscher wished to maintain the feeling of vegetation running wild and a sense of a secret undisturbed forest. So over a period of three years trees were felled and new ones planted in a natural way, views of a neighbouring churchyard were closed and the edge of the lake cleared and secured.

A source of inspiration has been the idea of the folly and in particular the garden of Bomarzo, north of Rome, which has grotesque carvings of giants' heads set into the hillside. The landscape architects have worked with the land artist Alfio Bonanno who has created a wonderful bridge and "bird's nest". For the future, grottos, bowers and plants made into figures are proposed. There is also an "opera house" made from the prow of a boat by the artist Anders Thygesen which survives from the 1978 garden.

Planting is in tune with the natural woodland: willow, beech, snowberry, bracken, honeysuckle, hop, ivy and grass are the main materials and bamboo and rhododendron have been introduced.

Knud Jensen, director of the Louisiana Museum, writes: "Children are not interested in adult visual art, though sometimes they pretend they are. Museums of art must co-operate with clever educators or with artists themselves to create works of art, in order to allow children to understand and use an artistic language, so giving them experience instead of education."

This lakeside garden is a place for children to lose themselves in such experiences.

The view of the Children's House and the adjacent Giacometti Hall (with steps in between) from the lake – note how the lake edge has been made safe.

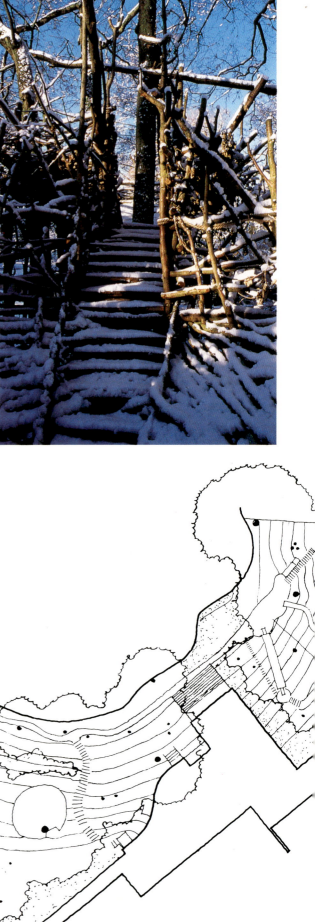

The bird's nest sculptural play piece by Alfio Bonanno.

42 Site plan.
The Children's House is on the right and children can descend by the steps to enjoy the lakeside gardens. The log bridge crosses the stream on the left.

Alfio Bonanno's bridge set
within woodland with the bird's
nest beyond in the trees.

A child's view of the
playground.

The view through the play area
from the playground towards
the grove of trees.

Swirling ultramarine, black, yellow and orange stripes of rubberized paving decorate the middle space.

Enclosures for running and
chasing and games of tag.

Kindergarten Birken III

Marktheidenfeld, Germany

Robin Winogrond

This is a children's playground which aims to offer a field of ideas beyond the range of standard children's play equipment. The challenge was to provide an outdoor environment for play which children could endow with their own stories, fantasies, wishes and meanings.

Robin Winogrond has merged the elements of play and their setting to create a place of play-theatre. The kindergarten and its playground (for three to six year olds) is set in a very hilly landscape on the edge of the small town of Marktheidenfeld, west of Würzburg; the site was formerly an apple orchard.

The playground consists of a series of straight grass terraces angled around and rising up from the curved kindergarten building (designed by Willi Müller). The site is naturally sloping, and terraces allowed the creation of a flat plaza at the lowest level close to the nursery school building. This building is itself subdivided radially, and the further lines of terraces, hedges, trees and the concrete walls in the steepest corner allowed a dialogue between the architecture and the play garden.

There are 12 ways, in the form of steps and ramps, by which children can go up and down the terraces. Constructions which are in part over-sized "toys" and

Above: Simple steel tubes become swings.

in part set designs have been placed on the terraces. Robin Winogrond has designed a series of contrasting play experiences whereby children show off, hide, construct things or just stretch and exercise themselves. For example, the "drawing fountain" consists of a 3 x 5-metre raised platform of slate with a sort of concrete door frame on one side through which a tube shoots a jet of water into the centre of the platform. Children can draw on the slate with chalk, and then wash away their drawings, or they can fill a recess in the centre of the platform by damming an outlet and create a shallow lake.

Simple steel tubes painted in primary colours become swings, and timber stockades serve for games of tag.

Winogrond draws on existentialism and, in particular, on the work of Cocteau as inspiration for her ideas. Places and landscape design can have meanings open to individual interpretation. This is landscape design as a setting for the choreography of play.

Site plan.

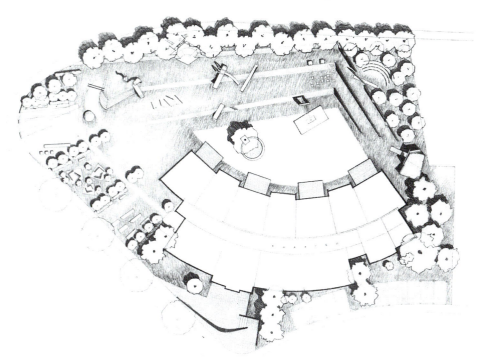

The Wendy House.

50

The red House of Wind
encircled by the overlapping
ramps of the Road of Wind.

Himeji Mitate Park

Himeji City, Hyogo, Japan

Mitsuru Man Senda, Environment Design Institute

This is an old park in the suburbs of Himeji, formerly used for teaching road skills. It has been transformed into a children's play park based on the designer's theory of circular play systems and observation of the game of tag. The aim was to create a place that would foster informal group interaction and play. It is a response to the growth of computer games and the excessive homework which increasingly make Japanese children stay indoors.

The space is enclosed by trees and is gently sloped so rainwater can drain away. There are two linked installations: the Kaze no Ie (House of Wind), approached by the Kaze no Michi (Road of Wind), and the Daichi no Michi (Road of Earth). They are in structural steel with preservative-treated Oregon pine decking. The design criteria were: provision of a circular route, safety, provision of high points, a certain amount of confusion, short cuts and enclosed spaces where several children can congregate, and finally "spatial porosity" or links between spaces.

The two structures rise from the hilltop grass. Kaze no Michi is a wooden ramp which forms a spiralling octagon and leads to the Kaze no Ie, built in red perforated steel sheet. Within the Kaze no Ie is a space furnished with ropes and a net to make a sort of jungle gym. Yellow steel handrails on the Daichi no Michi double as speaking tubes. This Road of Wind also leads across to the Daichi no Michi by a land bridge. The whole is an essay in orchestrating and provoking open-ended children's play.

Above: View of the Road of Earth in the distance with the Road of Wind in the foreground. The yellow rails are speaking tubes.

Right: Within the House of Wind is a sort of gym of ropes and nets.

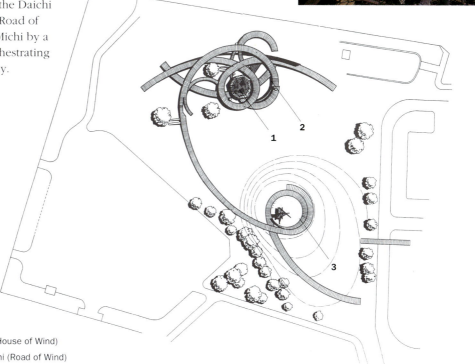

Plan

1 Kaze no Ie (House of Wind)

2 Kaze no Michi (Road of Wind)

3 Daichi no Michi (Road of Earth)

The sunken lake at night.

Kromhoutpark

Tilburg, The Netherlands

Bureau B + B

The beginning of the Climbing Line is a sort of moon gate set in this blue brick wall: the girl is balancing on the rope bridge over the lake.

Kromhoutpark is near the centre of Tilburg. It was formerly a parade ground for the military and B + B was commissioned in 1991 to make a public park. Unusually there was no strict design brief and so B + B responded by producing a design of infinite opportunities.

The site is rectangular and the surrounding streets are lined with row trees. The design consists of a rectangle within a rectangle. In the periphery the designers provided lawns for sports and games with three enclosed children's playgrounds.

Within the inner rectangle is a surprise, a sunken lake, also rectangular, with a curvaceous, irregularly shaped island accessed by a causeway and bridges. A band of evergreen bamboo and rhododendron encloses the sunken area and the lake to form a space within a space. Four paths form design "lines" radiating from the lake. Each line is furnished with play facilities and park furniture, and the paths lead to and connect with housing around the park. Two of the lines are for the active, the Water Line and the Climbing Line; two lines are for everyone, the Bridge and Art Lines. The Water Line zig-zags lightning-like with water flowing beneath steel grilles. Metre-high surprise fountains shoot up through the grilles, and the pathway leads to a causeway crossing the lake to the island in the middle. The Climbing Line is approached through a blue brick wall where a small, circular Moon Gate gives access to a hanging bridge. The line called The Bridge crosses both land and water on slender steel supports at metre intervals to give a feeling of lightness. Finally, the Art Line is represented by white arrowheads set into dark concrete and pointing to the island in memory of the original, abortive proposal for rows of columns surmounted by busts of local dignitaries.

This is design as a sort of playfulness, design by *homo ludens*: it is open-ended and particularly appropriate for a place of play and recreation.

The Bridge Line is set on an elegant, light timber and steel bridge.

54

The **Water Line** zig-zags lightning-like across the lake to the irregular curved island; to the right is the Bridge Line. The whole lake is sunken below the general level of the park.

The **Art Line** of white arrows set in dark concrete within a lake edge of crazy paving.

Early sketch plan. The lake in the middle, the varied routes beyond, which became the four "lines", and the perimeter of trees are the essence of this design of lines, routes, discovery and destination.

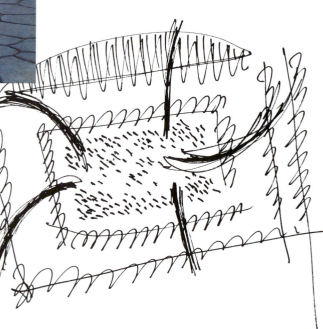

Coloured computer drawing. This is a park for everyone and the residents of Tilburg are challenged to discover the four "lines" to the island, represented in this drawing from the top clockwise as the Art Line, the Climbing Line, the Bridge Line and the zig-zagging Water Line, while the yellow path forms a fifth waterside edge. These "lines" and the water's edge are represented here three-dimensionally while the island, lake and the rest of the park are shown in two-dimensional plan.

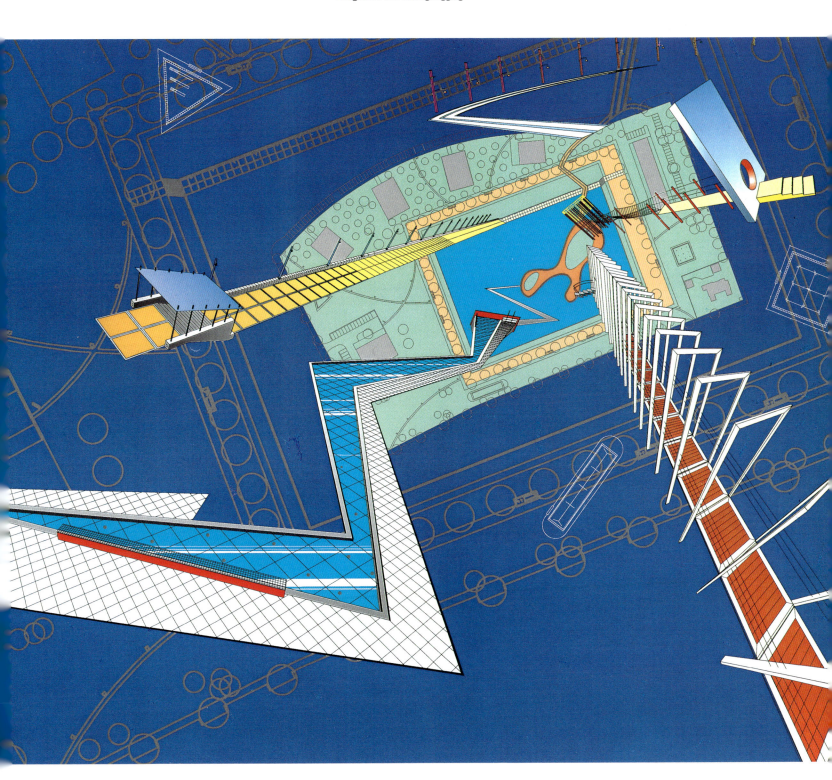

2.6

Weesner Family Amphitheater

Minnesota Zoological Gardens, Apple Valley, USA

Thomas Oslund of Hammel Green and Abrahamson

An amphitheatre set beside the Minnesota Zoo's lake and nestling into a stand of red oak – this is landscape architecture as a monumentalization of place. It is a design for an amphitheatre where families can view displays of trained birds of prey hunting and returning to their handler's gauntlet. Yet it is a design that is as much about choosing a site as it is about creating something new.

Minnesota Zoo is a natural landscape with lakes and woodland. The design balances the "natural" and the artificial: the setting is natural, a slope beside a wetland, the autumn colours of the red oaks behind and the flight of a bird of prey above, which, put together, create a drama. Within the amphitheatre there is artifice. The stage backdrop is of Minnesota Mankato-Kasota limestone, arranged rough cut in slabs over 5 metres high, and laid artificially as massive slivers of stone supported on a frame of 150 millimetre galvanized steel tubes and angles. This stone slab backdrop screens the bird rooms and offices behind, which are reached on one side by a footbridge.

The canopies rise overhead and the crowd looks down on the stage with its backdrop of limestone slabs.

The stage itself is a square of random cut limestone slabs. A smaller square pool slices diagonally across one corner, while above is a dead tree trunk (shades of Humphry Repton's planting here) which provides a perch. All this is set into a lawn of close-mown grass contrasting with the natural wetland beyond.

The amphitheatre, which seats 1,500 with extra standing room for 1,000, has limestone trim and redwood seats. It is set into the hillside and surmounted by a canopy of six separate hollow steel tubes supporting a Teflon-coated fibreglass membrane. Each section of the canopy is held up by a tubular steel truss and tied back by tension cables to the ground. Force and tension is poised so the whole structure seems about to take flight: the tubes and membrane recall a bird's wing. Indeed, the structure was modelled on the flight feathers of the condor.

57

Opposite: The amphitheatre at rest.

The lakeside setting at Minnesota Zoo.

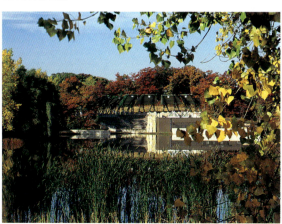

N

0   60'

Site plan

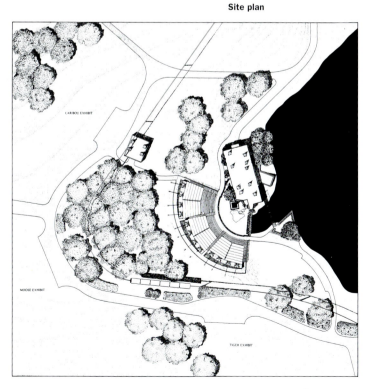

58

The cascade leading down to
the Water Garden.

2.7

Parc Terrasson-la-Villedieu

Terrasson, Dordogne, France

Kathryn Gustafson

This is potentially one of the great terrace gardens. Set on a hillside above the town of Terrasson-la-Villedieu, it is a park where the landscape almost becomes architecture and the architecture becomes park. It is an essay in land sculpture. In a forest of oaks on former agricultural terraces Kathryn Gustafson has used the linearity of the terraces to create great curves in the landscape.

This is a dialogue between nature and culture represented by the archetypical cultural forms: the meadow and the forest represent nature; the canal, the rose garden and the nursery represent mankind as cultivator; and the architectural elements – amphitheatre, the greenhouse, the paths and the embankments – represent man as constructor. The path through the park represents a voyage of discovery.

The visitor approaches from the main road and first sees a line of wind vanes on 12-metre high masts; each mast has a bell so one hears as well as sees the winds. This Axis of the Winds leads to the car-park and the entrance path. From here there is a *trompe l'oeil* perspective of waving high grass and white roses which leads upwards to the top of the park. The main pathway slopes upwards towards the *serre* or glasshouse by English architect Ian Ritchie and towards the Garden of Elements. To one side there is the site of a future nursery which will sell different varieties of plants used in the park. The Garden of Elements consists of four small gardens on the theme of plants – rhododendrons, Montpelier maple, ferns

The cruciform Water Garden with fifty jets creating rainbows in the sunlight.

and moss – which were chosen from the natural vegetation of the area. The *serre* is made with stone-filled gabion walls and a light glass structure by Ritchie and the structural engineer Henry Bardsley. It serves as bookshop, café and exhibition space. Above the *serre* is an outdoor amphitheatre set in the hillside.

The main path has views back over the town and leads on to the Rose Garden and Water Garden. The Rose Garden consists of a 1,000-square-metre suspended steel structure which floats over the hillside, and over which the roses will climb to form a floating tapestry. The Water Gardens are in the form of a cross with jets and are fed by a cascade coming down from the hillside. The public can wander here and explore the facets of water. On the nearby lawn is an "Ephemeral Tracing": a large-scale plan of a seventeenth-century European garden painted on the grass so that over the year it fades and is lost, to be replaced by another garden plan.

The return path leads through the "Sacred Forest" of oak where there are runnels and 50 bells are suspended from the trees. This is landscape design as poetry.

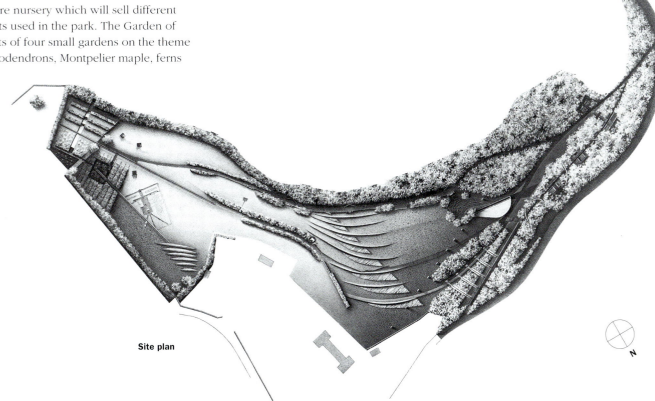

Site plan

N

Left: The Axis of the Winds
with wind vanes on masts

The view down to the Rose
Garden and the suspended
steel "tapestry" over which the
roses will grow.

Detail of the Water Garden.

The way through the forest with, in the background, the overhead golden ribbon that marks the way ahead.

The wall of the causeway is
inscribed with a quotation from
Hölderlin: "*Ihr holden
Schwäne/Tunkt ihr das Haupt*"
(You lovely swans/You dip
heads).

Three stele in the wood bear
inscriptions by Heidegger and
play on the German meaning of
the word "woodpath".

Schlosspark Grevenbroich

Grevenbroich, Nordrhein-Westfalen, Germany

Georg Penker/Ian Hamilton Finlay

This poetic castle park is set in the woods around Schloss Grevenbroich and was part of the 1995 Grevenbroich Landesgartenschau (Garden Festival). Its ambition is that constant theme in landscape design: the contrast between nature and civilization.

Formerly the woodland was pure stands of poplar on an 8 x 8-metre grid which Georg Penker has recast as a setting for the Scottish artist and poet Ian Hamilton Finlay's continuing dialogue on the meaning of place and poetry, of landscape and ideas. This is an intellectual landscape; the aim is a Gesamtkunstwerk, a total, united and complete collective work of art, involving Hamilton Finlay drawing on the ideas, emotions and words of a series of writers and thinkers and placing them in a landscape partially already existing and partially Penker's creation.

A visual and poetic enterprise, the landscape has become a small book: *Neun Vorschläge für einen Wald* (Nine Proposals for a Wood), published by Wild Hawthorn Press, which Hamilton Finlay runs from his house, Little Sparta, in the hills west of Edinburgh. So one proposal of Hamilton Finlay's given physical form by Penker is for an inscribed stone bench placed in a solitary spot between two trees. This is furnished with the quotation in German from Hérault de Séchelles: "*Gesellschaft heilt Stolz und Einsamkeit heilt Eitelkeit*" (society is the cure for pride and solitude for vanity).

The castle was built in the fourteenth century on an island in the River Erft surrounded by marshland. Today it is surrounded by the industrial town of Grevenbroich, between Cologne and Düsseldorf, and the landscape is dominated by open-cast coal mining supplying the town's two large, brown coal power stations.

The project involved restoration of part of the old bed of the River Erft by dredging, and freeing avenues of oak and beech from the competition of the poplar trees. Wild flowers and shrubs have been introduced to the woodland, in total some 70 native species and 200,000 plants.

An old fire station building has been restored as a youth centre and linked to the castle by a straight, 120-metre long granite slab path which runs over the lake and alongside a wedge-shaped lawn, carved out of the poplar woods. The collision of undulating woodland floor and flat lawn is marked by rippling concrete walls.

A pergola enters the wood and changes from regular carpentry to rustic branches.

All this provides a setting for Hamilton Finlay's conceits. The straight path connecting the fire station and castle crosses the lake on a causeway, the wall of which is inscribed with a quotation from Hölderlin: "*Ihr holden Schwäne/Tunkt ihr das Haupt*" (You lovely swans/You dip heads). A pergola "*Inter artes et naturam*" (Between art and nature) enters the wood and changes in form from regular carpentry to rustic branches; a solitary oak reminiscent of those in the paintings of Caspar David Friedrich is affixed with a quotation from Virgil's *Aeneid*: "*Iter mare prorumptum et/pelago pemit arva sonanti*" (The ocean's roar is heard /on the meadow of the land). Thus a landscape is reclaimed and given meaning: a seat is not a "sitting area" but becomes a place of contemplation.

63

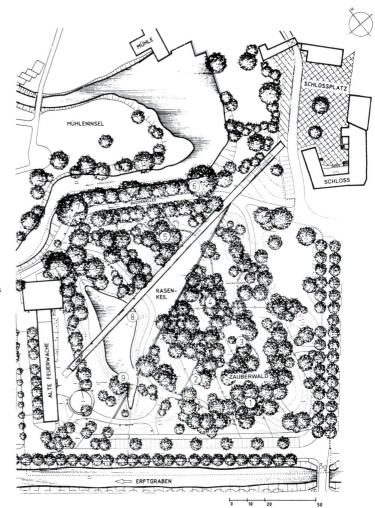

Site plan

1 Pergola
2 Bronze plaques
3 Pyramid
4 Rousseau busts
5 Vincennes signpost
6 Seat
7 Plaque on tree
8 Swan inscription
9 Plaque on tree

Spring tulips grow in beds lined with protective kerb stones. New York Public Library is in the background.

The crowded central lawn set below the cliff of Sixth Avenue in early spring. The promenade on the right has four rows of plane trees (Platanus acerifolia). The balustrade in the foreground is typical of the formal Beaux Arts design of this park.

Bryant Park

New York, USA

Hanna/Olin Ltd

By the 1970s Bryant Park off Fifth Avenue and next to New York Public Library was a place of muggings and drug dealing. The park had been redesigned in 1934 in a formal French style which raised and isolated it from the street and enclosed it with railings, hedges and balustrades.

Hanna/Olin were appointed in 1986 to rescue and rehabilitate the park. As landscape architects they were an appropriate choice because of their Beaux Arts sympathies: they had previously worked on Battery Park City in New York and in 1986 had just begun the design of Canary Wharf in London. However, the challenge at Bryant involved much more than merely style. Led by Laurie Olin, the design team included a sociologist, three architects, a garden designer, lighting consultant and engineer.

Their strategy was twofold: social engineering and landscape design change interrelated. The social engineering covers programmes of attracting park users and so embraces new amenities, including flower and book stalls, discount ticket booths, concession stands and a series of events ranging from concerts to fashion events, film festivals, political rallies and parties. Two new restaurants are currently proposed. Maintenance was changed to allow full-time staffing; four security guards were taken on with both day- and night-time patrols and toilets are regularly monitored. And the park is closed at night to prevent vandalism and crime.

The social engineering has been linked to a programme of design approaches. These included the opening up of sightlines by removing balustrades and hedges, the widening of existing entrances and provision of new entrances mid-block on both 40th and 42nd streets, ramps to give access for the disabled, new kiosks and toilets, new flower borders and a central lawn, and provision of one thousand movable chairs. There is a new lighting scheme which includes 20 bronze lamp standards modelled on those designed by Carrere & Hastings for the New York Public Library. Elsewhere the traditional bishop's crook fittings provide footpath lighting around the park, and rooftop floodlights were positioned on the 45th storey of the New York Telephone building across the Avenue of the Americas to give a "moonglow" effect. The aim of the lighting scheme was to be appropriate but not too strong: overbright lighting can induce insecurity. Tree surgeons inspected all the existing trees and there is a

programme of new tree planting, while intensive amenity horticulture and irrigation was reintroduced.

Aesthetic improvements alone could not rescue the park: it had to function socially and therefore maintenance, security and events organization went hand in hand with design. Continuing finance was organized by means of establishing the Bryant Park Restoration Corporation funded by a special business district tax of 11 cents per square foot per annum. This contributes $850,000 towards the $1.2 million annual running costs, and the balance comes from business concession with $250,000 from the City Parks Department.

The result is like a catalyst, leading to public and business confidence in the whole area. As the *New York Times* said: "Bryant Park is good for New York; what's good for New York is good for America."

Plans

1 Existing formal and symmetrical Beaux Arts layout.

2 Reinforced by Hanna/Olin in this controlled and formal drawing.

1

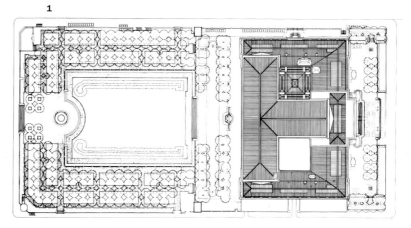

2

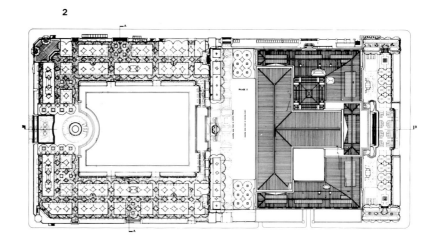

Columns and a low cascade
into the moat mark the edge of
the entrance plaza.

Niigata Prefecture Museum of Modern Art

Nagaoka City, Niigata Prefecture, Japan

Shunmyo Masuno

Shunmyo Masuno's Museum of Modern Art in Niigata uses the river as a starting point to explore the ways in which man can live in harmony with nature. This is pure Zen: Masuno is both landscape architect and Zen Buddhist priest – trained at Sojii Temple – and the practice of *ropparamitsu*, which is the Buddhist ethos of making one's way in an ideal world, suffuses his work.

The museum is situated along the Shinano River and is a point of contact between Nagaoka City and the open countryside beyond. The building is dug into the ground, creating the impression that it has grown naturally from the earth. Roof gardens face the river. Cars are set to the south and the building rises in terraces up from the car-park. At the building curtilage is a landscape of slabs and water channels which form moats at the edge of the simple, diagonally banded entrance plaza in Chinese

granite and brick. Trees by the entrance are chestnut (*Aesculus turbinata* Blume) underplanted with periwinkle (*Vinca minor*).

On the river side of the building, planting includes trees such as *Zelkova serrata* Makino and *Populus* (*xeuro-americana*), as well as groundcover plants and over 30 species of low trees and shrubs such as *Mazus miquelii* Makino, *Albiflorus* Makino, *Aubrietia deltoidea*, *Phlox subulata* and *Lysimachia nummullaria*. This wild and "natural" landscaping is in direct contrast to the formal entrance of the museum.

The roof of the building becomes grass and terrace walls; wide and expansive vistas open towards and "borrow" the landscape of the mountains beyond: the transition between city and nature is made.

67

Site plan.

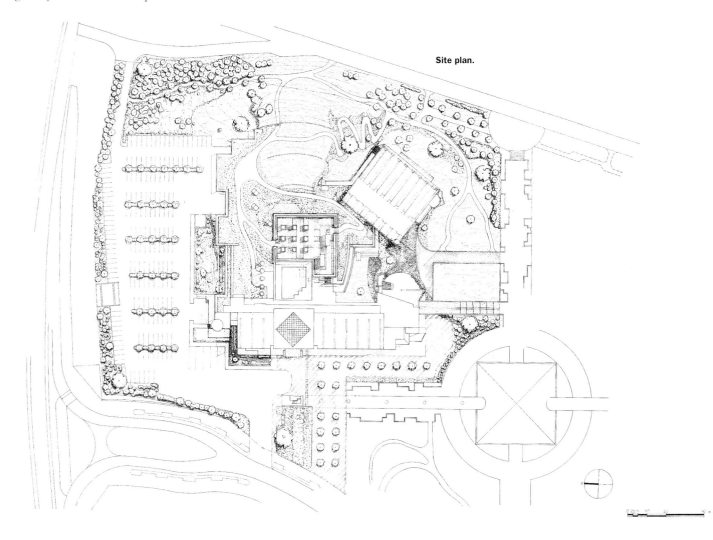

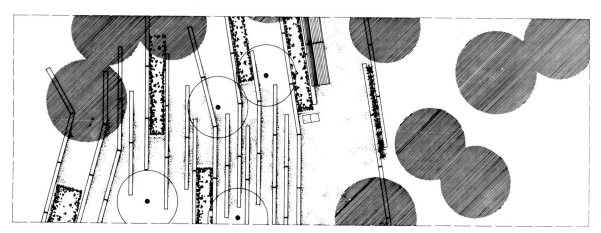

A cross-section of the terrace steps shows the interplay of linear terraces and informal planting.

The lakeside promenade and the ramped bridge which connects town and park.

The waterfall behind which
people can walk or sit and
admire the view through the
cascade of water.

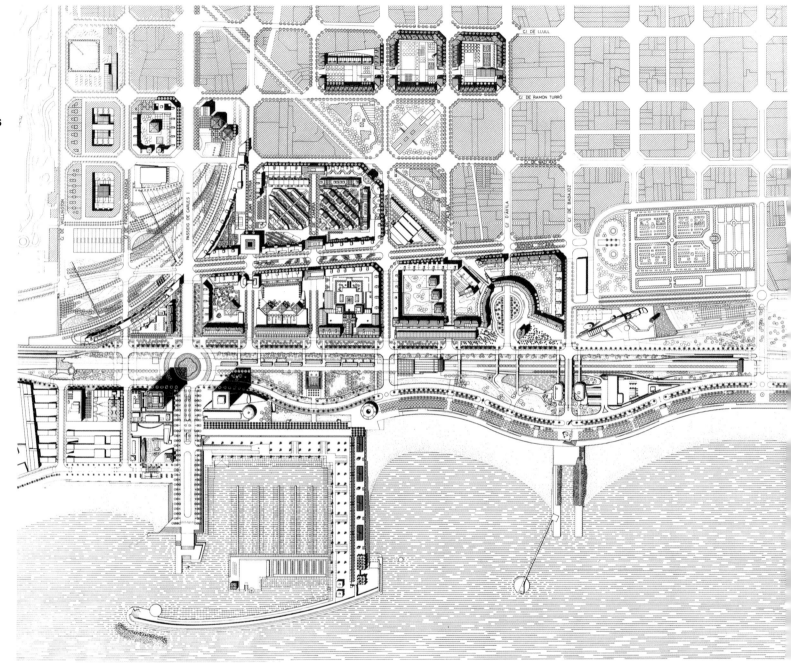

Site plan. The Olympic Village
is above the straight highway
alignment that passes under
the three sections of the park.
The sections are (from the
left): Parc de les Cascades,
Parc del Port and, to the right
where the highway emerges
from tunnel, the Parc d'Icària.

Left: Antoni Llena's sculpture of David (David i Goliat) dominates the central route through the Parc de les Cascades.

Below (top): The colonnades in the Parc del Port.

Below (bottom): Weeping willows (*Salix babylonica*) and green lawns line the lake in the Parc d'Icària.

Below (left): The Parc d'Icària lake with its wooden overbridges.

Curved and planted canal in August 1991, the year before opening.

Computer graphics

1. Green: the new forest; light brown: urban area after 1992; dark brown: permanent park after 1992.

2. The essential canal drainage system.

3. The essential canal drainage system and the extension of the system. The extension was necessary to get soil material for·the dike in the middle.

4. Emphasizing the landscape pattern by the use of rows of poplars.

1

2

3

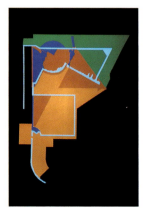

4

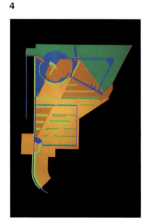

2.13
Floriade

The Hague-Zoetermeer, The Netherlands

Michiel den Ruijter

Every ten years the Dutch hold a Floriade (garden festival). The 1992 Floriade took place just south of The Hague in the new town of Zoetermeer. These Dutch garden festivals are long-term affairs as regards their preparation and planning and the design, which involves a commitment to the long-term afteruse of the site.

Zoetermeer won the competition for the garden festival in 1985, and the scheme involved in effect three plans: firstly, for a park and regional forest; secondly, for the garden festival exhibition, which lasted six months in 1992; and thirdly, for Rokkeveen West, a new housing area being built on part of the garden festival area. The Floriade site area was 68 hectares with a further 25 hectares of forestry, part of a total of 600 hectares of new forest between Zoetermeer and Delft to the west. Thirty hectares of the Floriade have become permanent parkland. The site is south of the Zoetermeer railway line and the E30 The Hague-Utrecht motorway and was formerly agricultural polder. A new railway station was built for Zoetermeer next to a motorway junction, and station and road junction both lead to the eastern end of the Floriade site and to car-parking. Beyond this was a great square, the Gansevoetplein, which was the base of a *pâte d'oie* from which three axial lines crossed the polder. The two outer axes formed the edge of a huge equilateral triangle. The central axis became a 3.5-metre high dike followed by a monorail which terminated in an 80-metre high observation tower. The northern axis was a flower walk with a vintage electric tramway to move visitors, and the third, southern axis followed a canal to a lake which filled the south-western apex of the triangle.

The lake expanded across the triangle to partially fill a great circle at this point. The circle was completed by a canal in its landward portion, and land also crossed water in the form of a chain of islets each planted with a willow tree (*Salix alba tristis*). The site was further subdivided by regular canals and lines of poplar trees planted like telegraph poles, bare rooted, in 1986.

Regular geometry is characteristic of Dutch landscape architecture and the Dutch landscape. In the Floriade masterplan this approach has been elevated to an almost democratic level in that the arrangment attempted to provide choice and equality of position. No position in the garden festival was intended to rank first; all were intended to appear equal, hence the use of the forms of the equilateral triangle and the circle. Contrasting with these regular forms was a series of changing curves and a meandering canal.

There were seven theme areas: the Entrance Area; Production and Engineering; The Consumer; The Environment; Future and Science; The World, with international theme gardens; Recreation. It is of the nature of garden festivals that planning has to be open-ended because there are changes in who will exhibit and provide theme gardens up until the last minute. So of the above theme areas only the Entrance Area, with its exhibition halls, and The Environment area could be planned in detail early on. The great axial routes and enclosure, such as the lines of poplars or mounds and dikes and canals, were the means of articulating the overall festival to avoid a cacophony of competing theme gardens. The Environment area was intended to be permanent and so was devoted to polder habitats. A series of sharp triangular mounds penetrate a canal edge and give rise to a range of varying dry and wet habitats.

The Floriade lasted from 10 April to 15 October 1992 and there were 3.4 million visitors. The central portion of the festival park is to be housing and this will be completed in 1997. What is significant is that the urban design is landscape-led, and the garden festival has produced a permanent legacy for Zoetermeer in the form of the parkland retained and the urban forestry. Now the Dutch are planning their next Floriade in 2002, to be in the Haarlemmermeer, between Schiphol Airport and Amsterdam.

Computer graphics continued

5 Introducing the asymmetrical goosefoot (pâte d'oie); the middle as a dike; the southern axis as a canal; the northern axis as a temporary flower axis.

6 The internal transport on top of the middle axis to avoid congestion in the narrow entrance area.

7 Introducing the pedestrian walkways in the direction of the land divisions of the original landscape.

5

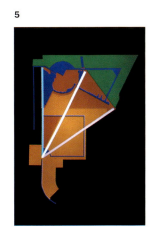

6

7

80

Detailed overview during the Floriade in 1992. In the foreground to the left are the triangular mounded polder habitat gardens. In the background is Zoetermeer New Town with, to the right, a new office development associated with the Floriade.

The new forest (bottom right) and the great circular lake, observation tower and monorail in the middle distance.

View of the theme gardens a
year before opening.

Typical view across the
gardens in 1992.

2.14

Parc Nus de la Trinitat
(Trinitat Cloverleaf Park)

Barcelona, Spain

Batlle i Roig, Arquitectes

The Parc Nus de la Trinitat occupies a motorway cloverleaf junction on the north-east edge of Barcelona. To the north are views of the hills around Vallbon and all about are housing, industry and railway lines. To the east is the canalized River Besos (the cloverleaf junction is on the site of a former meander of the river that had later become allotments and railway marshalling yards). Electricity pylons march across the skyline following the river. It is a no-man's land and typical urban fringe.

The park's location, however, on the line of the traditional approach to Barcelona from the north, also makes it a gateway to the city. So the design had to recognize its role as a gateway while also serving the local community of Trinitat. The designers aimed to minimize the effects of vehicle noise and the visual impact of the cars.

The design started with the land: it is an alluvial site bounded by the hard geology of rock which emerges around the edge of the flood plain to form a 9-metre high shelf. The roads have been located on the top of this shelf making a wall 15 metres high in total, and the majority of the park lies within and below the loop of roads.

It is a design based on linearity. The immediate precedents are the river, the electricity lines and the railway lines, but the new green lines are vegetation of a scale and massing equal to a motorway intersection and forming a curve reminiscent of the old river meander. Such lines of trees in the landscape also recall the orchards and roadside avenues one sees passing through the Catalan countryside when approaching Barcelona from the Pyrenees.

**Above and opposite:
Lines of olives and
ranks of poplar trees
set out along the edge
of the formal lake.**

Park users can enter at the lowest level via a metro station and then by pedestrian subway connections to the housing around the park. A large, formal lake edged with poplars (*Populus nigra italica*) follows the line of an esplanade which ends in a great rank of steps and an amphitheatre. Containing the curve of the esplanade is a gleaming white terrace wall above which are tennis courts and a pelota pitch. Above is a plaza which rises to bridge a section of motorway to provide a direct link to housing on the north-west. Within the centre of the park, curving terraces of meadow and lines of *Punica granatum*, cherry (*Prunus cerasifera pissardii*), Leyland cypress (*Cupressocyparis leylandii*) and poplar (*Populus euroamerica*) mass against the skyline and are visible from the roads around. Old olive trees (*Olea europaea*) have been transplanted to make similar flowing linear orchards.

The challenge of the project was to make somewhere out of nowhere, and this is a scheme that contains a universal lesson for major cities worldwide.

The highway junction made a park. The roads are the Barcelona eastern ring road, Cintura del Litoral (top of photograph); the N152, which leads to France (mid left); and the main railway line to France crosses the site. The road bridge at the top left crosses the dry bed of the River Besos.

The large formal lake follows
the curve of the roads and
ends in a great rank of steps.

84

Given such strong linear
elements as the roads, river
and railway, the challenge for
the park designers was to
create something equally
powerful. This they did by
forming new linear masses of
vegetation to rival the
transport lines.

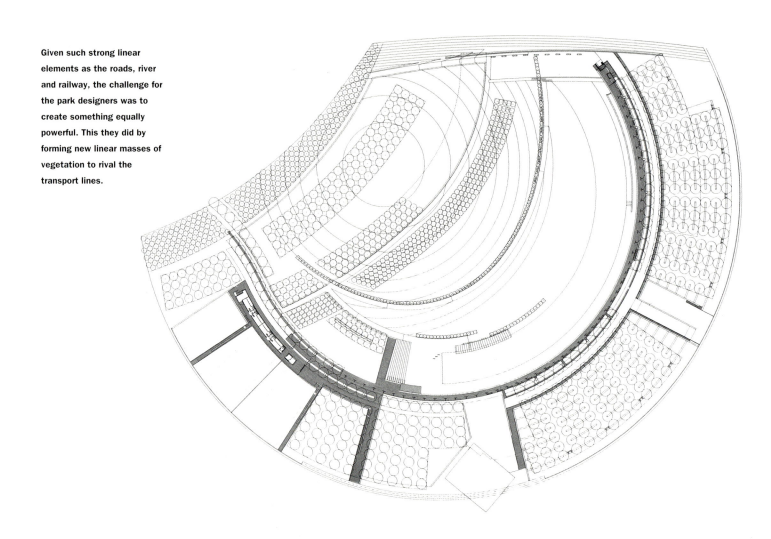

Terraces are pure architectonic
form.

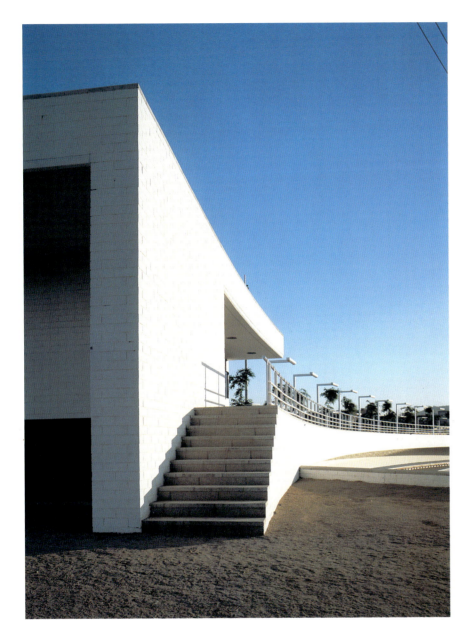

Strong colours contrast with
the gleaming white painted
brick walls.

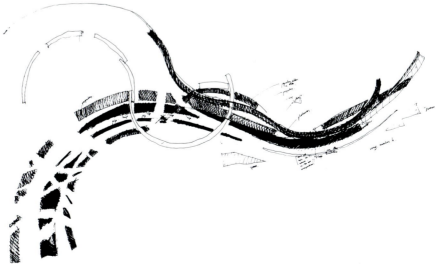

Plan of the vegetation.

Uppermill Cemetery

Saddleworth, Greater Manchester, UK

Camlin Lonsdale

This cemetery was commissioned by a small rural parish in the southern Pennine Hills. It is set on marginal land at the edge of enclosed pastureland and open moorland. The cemetery serves as an open space for local residents and hill walkers.

Robert Camlin drew on two sources of inspiration. The first was the existing site. Broad belts of indigenous woodland were planted along the contours in order to draw in the surrounding countryside and enclose a number of small upland meadows. The characteristic Pennine drystone walls of gritstone were used and the stone was also used for the paths and symbolic sculptural features.

The second design source was the idea of the ceremony or dignity of the cemetery as a reflection of the formality with which people approach bereavement. This embraced the awareness of external or "infinite" forces including time and spirituality and furthermore the need for comfort, compassion and well-being and the desire for tangible references.

The idea of infinity was represented by an infinite axis expressed as an avenue leading to views of distant countryside. The awareness of movement along this avenue is marked by pairs of drystone niches where the axis passes through the three tree belts. The niches each contain a specimen yew tree and together form three gateways along the axis which link the avenue and the woodland. The avenue begins in a square with a single yew tree, and in its lowest corner a flight of steps leads to the existing footpath. There is in addition a "Finite Axis" marked by wooden obelisks, keystone boundary markers in the drystone boundary walls and stone bollards that also mark out parking bays.

Between infinite and finite, intangible and tangible is a conceptual break which is expressed in the design by "The Wall". The entrance area on the east of The Wall is marked by a symmetrical arrangement of footpaths, parking area and avenues of pine trees to give an order and dignity to the entrance to the cemetery. On the west side of The Wall the meadows and belts of woodland are laid out in a more organic and ephemeral way. The Wall is broken in several places to symbolize the range of thresholds between these two types of landscape: parts of The Wall are arranged as if in decay and other sections are displaced to one side.

Opposite: The path and gate in summer.

87

The plan with three woodland belts, the Infinite Axis and the Finite Axis, and the entrance area.

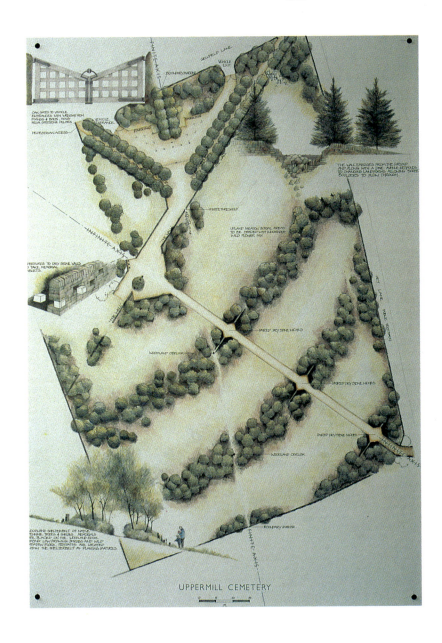

UPPERMILL CEMETERY

88

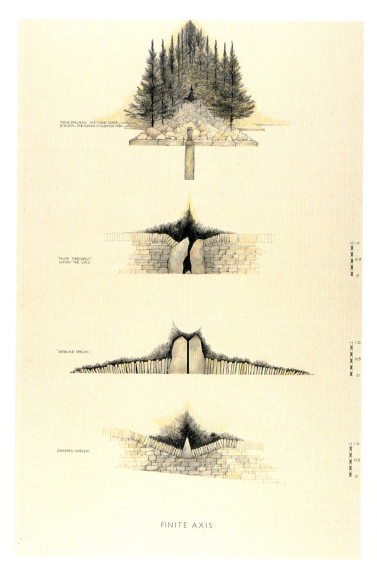

FINITE AXIS

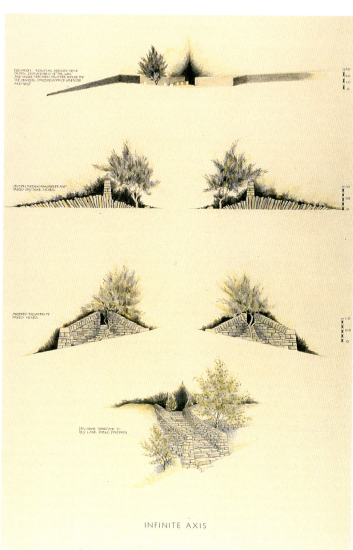

INFINITE AXIS

Robert Camlin's drawings of the axes.

The view out to distant landscapes from the Infinite Axis.

Drystone walls are part of the character of this landscape.

Joondalup Central Park, Perth, Western Australia is set in a dry savannah landscape and the bush (and many existing trees) has been retained (see page 99). Intensive areas such as the lawns of the main lake are irrigated and contrast with the dry savannah.

3 Ecology & Conservation

Nocturnal view of the northern landfall with lines of white cockle shells and dark mussel shells.

3.1

Shell Project

Oosterschelde, Zeeland, The Netherlands

West 8 Landscape Architects

Below: The view from the road. The lines tend to create an interference pattern.

Bottom: Detail of the light and dark shells.

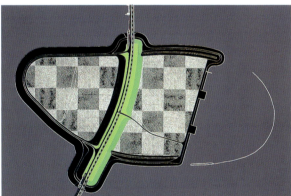

The design for the whole scheme of disappearing shell patterns.

93

Following the 1953 floods in The Netherlands, the mouth of the River Scheldt has been protected by a vast scheme of dams and barrages. The Rijkswaterstaat (Ministry of Waterways and Public Works) commissioned West 8 to create artificial dunes on the construction islands, docks and sand dumps left over after these delta works were completed in 1985.

A major road runs along the barrage and West 8 aimed to create a design on a scale that would register when viewed from cars travelling fast, to open views to the North Sea and to create a landscape design that would enhance the ecological value of the area.

The sand dumps were shaped into large plateaux which were covered with shells, a waste product of the fishing industry in nearby Yerseke. Shells, of course, form the nesting grounds for sea birds; dark shells attract dark birds and light-coloured shells likewise light birds because of the advantage of camouflage. So the plateaux were covered with 3-centimetre layers of dark and light shells in strong patterns. White cockle shells (*Cerastoderma edulis*) attract white herring gulls and the dark blue mussel shells (*Mytilus edulis*) attract black oystercatchers. The shells were intended to be laid in a chequerboard pattern covering the island of Roggenplaat (this is to be carried out in 1997), and at the southern landfall of the barrage diagonal stripes crossed towards the road to create an interference pattern at speed.

The essence of this project is its use of process. It is transitory: in five years the thin layers of shells disappear and the area becomes dune land. The design manipulates formal geometry and is based on ecological principles to create bold "artificial" patterns in the landscape in tune with natural processes. The effects are striking but in no way counter to nature. This rigorous yet understanding approach, based on true ecological values rather than the mere appearance of natural form, is typical of the new Dutch landscape architecture at its provocative best.

Parque Ecologico Xochimilco

Mexico City, Mexico

Grupo de Diseño Urbano

In Aztec times Mexico City was effectively an island surrounded by five lakes, and food was grown on chinampas, oblong plots reclaimed from the shallow lake bottoms. By the twentieth century, only portions of three of the lakes survived (lakes Texcoco, Zumpango and Xochimilco), and the area of chinampas had been reduced until they only remained by Lake Xochimilco (pronounced so-chee-meel-co), where they are known for flower production, most especially of dahlias. In the 1970s this area came under further threat when the city began pumping ground water from below Lake Xochimilco while dumping sewage into the canals which surround and provide access to the chinampas. The sewage led to the growth of water hyacinth, which blocked the canals, and the whole ecosystem was in danger of being lost.

However, the area achieved Unesco "World Heritage" status in 1987 and, prompted by this, 3,000 hectares of land around the lake are being conserved. Two water treatment plants now clean the sewage water before it enters the canal system and 200 kilometres of canals have been cleared of water hyacinth. Some 1,100 hectares of chinampas have been restored and flower production is flourishing.

Parque Xochimilco is a 278-hectare area which serves as a regional park for Mexico City. It consists of a 54-hectare central lagoon and bird reserve, a chinampa demonstration area and a botanical garden, a 68-hectare sports park and a flower and plant market. The area is bisected by the Anillo Perifico, Mexico City's ring road, although the carriageways have been separated to reduce the impact.

GDU, a group of architects, has designed a visitor centre which includes a museum of archaeology, botany and ethnology and a rooftop observation platform or mirador. The visitor centre faces the lake across a plaza covered with squares of grass from which rises a water tower in the form of an Archimedes' screw. This tower is repeated on the other side of the Anillo Perifico. Seven vegetated "jetties" project into the lake from the visitor centre plaza and there are also several footpath circuits in red paving which reach the edges of the lake. One main route passes through chinampa demonstration plots and is covered by a pergola, the Paseo de las Flores. Along the shoreline are moored rows of trajineras, the local flat-bottomed punts in yellow, red and blue that are used to ferry visitors. There are also

cycle rental facilities and a road train. There are up to 20,000 visitors a day at peak weekends.

The visitor centre is on the east of the ring road and on the west side there are separate car-park facilities for the flower market and the sports fields. The two main car-parks are linked by a pedestrian bridge across the two carriageways of the ring road. The flower market is a major facility consisting of 1,800 stalls arranged in rows around a rectangular plaza with services. The sports fields are screened by grass berms.

The works were carried out by a number of government agencies, including Mexico City Public Works Department and the Mexican army. This is a major attempt to conserve traditional cultivation and a natural resource in one of the largest expanding cities of the world. It seeks to reconcile the pressures of nature conservation with tourism by providing Lake Xochimilco with a status which will protect it. This is a continuing experiment and GDU has attempted to give it form and focus.

Opposite: The Archimedes' Screw Tower seen from the visitor centre.

Below: The visitor centre, also designed by Grupo de Diseño Urbano.

Left: Lake Xochimilco from the
plaza in front of the visitor centre.

Left: The lake and the
chinampas.

The Archimedes' Screw Tower
and the vegetated jetties
projecting into the lake.

Site plan

Paths of local stone meander through the irrigated lawns of the recreation area.

N

Site plan

Joondalup Central Park

Joondalup, Perth, Western Australia

Tract

Joondalup is a newly developing town which is planned to have a population of 250,000 by 2020. It is 26 kilometres north of Perth, about 5 kilometres from the coast and at an altitude of 50 metres. The Central Park links the railway station and civic centre to Lake Joondalup, which is part of the Yellagonga Regional Park.

The park forms a great wedge penetrating to the heart of the city and its design is a composition based on an interplay between the new settlement and the existing landscape. Its boundaries are delineated by the straight blocks of the city's grid plan and the two dual carriageway highways, Grand Boulevard and Lakeside Drive, which cross the park. The impact of Grand Boulevard has been minimized by separating each carriageway and by traffic calming. This road serves as a drop-off point for the central, western end of the park, which is predominantly urban plaza, serving future department stores and the railway station. Lakeside Drive crosses the park on embankment, and park paths and the stream, which is a main feature, both pass under the road.

The park, which will total 20 hectares, was formerly bushland, and the design aims to retain the heathland and Jarrah and Banksia woodland species. It is also a dry, savanna landscape with a low rainfall and with poor limestone soil, so one element in the park consists of areas of natural bushland, none of which is irrigated and from which the public is excluded. Natural regeneration is encouraged in the areas of natural ecosystems that form a framework for the whole park. Within this framework of natural spaces are set irrigated recreation areas. The water comes from boreholes and has a high iron content, so water features such as weirs act as aerators and, together with ozone filters, remove the iron.

The completed design will include urban plazas at the western end of the park, and a grassed oval common close to the civic centre with a cross-axial connection to a new formal curved lake. Next to the Wanneroo Council building there is an amphitheatre, and from there long "ridings" or cleared vistas lead through the bush to the lake edge where a performance deck and landings are planned. Near the lake and alongside the stream indigenous Australian wetland vegetation such as the endangered red cedar has been planted.

One theme of the project has been to celebrate native Australian materials, plants, animals and culture. Limestone walls and granite paths and concrete paviors of local aggregate are used generally and there is a programme of furnishing the park with bronze sculptures of native animals such as the water beetle, western swamps tortoise and banjo frogs.

So far the first 2.5-hectare stage of the park has been constructed and planted. The scheme is of interest because of the effort made to retain existing natural landscape in the centre of a new city and to devise a form of park particular and appropriate to Western Australia.

Below: An irrigated recreation lawn set within a backdrop of native bush.

Bottom: The straight promenade is a diagonal cut across the curvilinear forms of the park and connects it to the railway station.

Night view of the central area
with reception, bar, restaurant
and swimming pool.

Seven Spirit Wilderness

Arnhem Land, Northern Territory, Australia

EcoSystems

The Garig National Park is on the coast of the Northern Territory just 11 degrees south of the equator. Set within it and some 100 kilometres east of Darwin is the Cobourg Peninsula. In 1987 the Cobourg Peninsula Sanctuary Board decided to permit a tourist development in keeping with the Aboriginal owners' special relationship with their environment and as an additional source of income. EcoSystems first advised the board on the choice of site and then worked with the chosen developer to create a low-impact tourist development.

The site is on the top of small cliffs with views over the sandy beaches of Coral Bay both to east and west; the cliffs also give protection against cyclone-induced storm surge. The site is well drained and this allowed construction traffic to operate in the wet season. It has variable soils ranging from deeper pockets supporting dense forest to poorer lateric soils supporting grass and shrubs. But generally the site is open forest, which is attractive for a resort because it allows sea breezes to penetrate.

This is a tourist resort with no golf courses or tennis courts and no swimming in the sea due to the danger of sharks and crocodiles. The tourist activities are intended to be low-impact: bird watching, fishing, photography, and walking and exploring the mangrove swamps, lagoons, dunes and associated grassland. There are 24 guest houses with a total capacity of about 50 and a central area with reception, lounge, bar, restaurant and swimming pool. The guest houses are set in the woodland with secluded open-air bathrooms. Visitors reach the resort by boat from Port Easington.

EcoSystems' contribution involved site selection, environmental impact assessment and site survey, followed by site planning and control of construction work. The site planning aimed to use existing surface drainage by directing water from access tracks and cut-off drains to be discharged over hard rocks and through thick vegetation into the natural drainage lines. Construction areas were sited so as to minimize damage to vegetation, and buildings were located amongst existing vegetation which screens them. The buildings are in neutral colours, with dark-brown timber and light-grey pitched roofs. Service trenches were located only along access tracks and construction was controlled by fences. At the end of construction there was a clean-up operation; soil affected by construction, for example, was dug up

and replaced with stockpiled soil, with the contaminated soil being used for maintenance work on the access tracks. The construction camp has been redeveloped as fruit and vegetable gardens. Continuing care and maintenance is of course vital to this tropical paradise garden. The project is a prime example of how landscape architecture can minimize the impact of appropriate tourist development and can reveal and conserve an extremely attractive natural habitat, in a way that helps support an Aboriginal rural economy.

Below: The central area in the daytime.
Bottom: The man-made and the natural merge.

Buildings are set informally and discreetly in the areas of open forest. Light-grey roofs and dark-brown timber structures were chosen for their neutral, recessive qualities.

Plan showing the site layout.

1 Social hub/habitat centre
2 Manager's residence
3 Staff house
4 Laundry
5 Maintenance shed and water tank
6 Barge landing
7 Workshop, generator and fuel storage

N

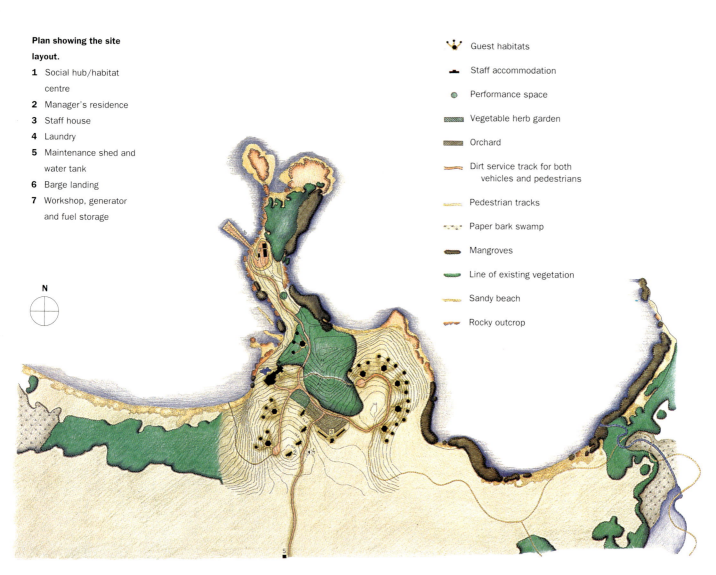

Guest habitats

Staff accommodation

Performance space

Vegetable herb garden

Orchard

Dirt service track for both vehicles and pedestrians

Pedestrian tracks

Paper bark swamp

Mangroves

Line of existing vegetation

Sandy beach

Rocky outcrop

ral area in its forest setting.

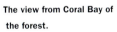

The view from Coral Bay of
the forest.

104

Fish ponds line the foot of the valley side.

Center for Regenerative Studies

Pomona, California, USA

John Lyle and Ronald Izumita

The Center for Regenerative Studies (CRS) at California State Polytechnic University is a communal environment for research, education and demonstration of regeneration or land reclamation as part of a long-term programme of ecological sustainability. John Lyle here aims to counter the view of Los Angeles as an anti-ecological city.

Lyle has taught at Cal Poly since 1968 and is known for his book *Design for Holistic Ecosystems* (Van Nostrand, 1985). Ecological ideas of energy and material cycles are fundamental to his approach to landscape design. At the Spadra landfill of the Los Angeles Sanitation Department Lyle has established the CRS using land as a medium for recycling. The idea for the CRS began in 1975 with a Cal Poly first-year design project looking at a self-sufficient university college. Inspired by his students, Lyle proposed the scheme be taken up by his university. At first it seemed doubtful, but when the Sanitation Department proposed a land swap, deeding 137 hectares to Cal Poly in exchange for permission for a refuse landfill on other university land, Cal Poly adopted Lyle's eco-village idea.

So now solar-powered buildings stand on a hillside while above them dumper trucks carry rubbish. The project is long term, at least ten years, and the first phase was completed in September 1994. It houses 20 students and will grow to a community of 80. The student residents grow food, generate energy, control their interior environments, recycle waste and manage the flow of water. As Lyle explains: "The central idea was integration of people and landscape in a human ecosystem which can function in a regenerative way, that is without depleting resources or causing pollution or diminishing the integrity of natural processes."

The challenges were those of dealing with a rigid and hierarchical university bureaucracy, overcoming inapplicable regulatory requirements, applying ecological principles to a range of life-supporting systems, expressing the whole idea in a formal way and giving free rein to the knowledge and ideas of a diverse group of some ten experts.

Buildings are constructed in knotty cedar and are solar heated and cooled (Lyle is both landscape architect and architect). They line the main street like a Wild West town. Pergolas shade the sidewalks and as in real Westerns there are no cars in the street. Fish ponds line the hillside as in a medieval monastery,

Electric buggies provide some transport around the village.

and the centre of the community is the equivalent of a refectory. Ultimately there will be grain on the hilltops, terraced planting beds for crops, and forestry on the steepest slopes; the fish ponds and horticulture are in the valley bottom close to the village.

The site has a heavy clay soil which is being improved with sewage sludge. Terraces are built with old tyres, and the compost heap is in full view of the buildings. This is an approach to landscape architecture that questions the usual ideas of neat and tidy places; it is a place of questioning and change, of self-sufficiency and learning. This is landscape architecture for the real world; as Lyle says: "I'm trying to get sustainability out of the fringe and into the mainstream."

Plan showing the different land uses

The valley
Bottomlands 1 hectare

Knoll tops
Upland grain 1 hectare

Bases of the knolls
Planting beds 1,600 square metres

Human use area
The village 0.9 hectares

Knoll sides
Terraced slopes 1.4 hectares

Steep slopes
Agroforestry 2 hectares

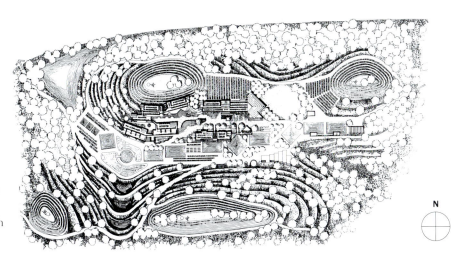

N

The village at the Center: the timber buildings have solar power and the use of cars is discouraged.

106

Vegetation is everywhere, even on the rooftops, and pergolas provide shade.

Crop terraces are made of
old tyres.

Buildings line the main street
like a Wild West town.

The Blue Pool where the

underground river emerges.

3.6

The Taung Monument

North West Province, South Africa

Environmental Design Partnership

This scheme is on the base of an escarpment on the edge of the Kalahari Desert. It was here during limestone quarrying that the "Child Skull" was discovered in 1925. The 2.5-million-year-old skull is evidence of earliest mankind. Subsequently, much less ancient Stone Age relics were also discovered. Mining ceased in 1977.

In 1985, on the sixtieth anniversary of the find, the then Bophithatswana President, Lucas Mangope, declared that the 1,400-hectare site should be protected as a nature reserve and this was later confirmed by tribal resolution. The North West Parks Board now administers the site.

The Environmental Design Partnership was appointed in 1989 to prepare an environmental appraisal of a 170-hectare study area. This led to the commission to plan the development of the area for research, education and recreation, and to promote the natural and scenic assets of the area. One concern was to create local employment opportunities; in this respect the project, though in a vastly different landscape, is similar to the tourist development of the Seven Spirit Wilderness in Australia (see page 101).

The designers' tasks included rehabilitating the old quarry areas and reusing the old mine buildings as a museum of mining history. Tourist and recreational improvements involved the creation of nature trails, sites for braai (barbecues) and picnics, and caravan and camping areas, and improving the environment of Buxton Village where unemployment had been high since the closure of the quarries.

The landscape works involved stabilization of steep slopes, and planting to reduce the glare from the white tufa. The Free State Botanical Garden supplied over 5,000 indigenous trees and 4 hectares were seeded using local grasses. Game-proof fences were erected to protect the new planting from domestic beasts and wildlife ("Taung" means "place of the lion" in Tswana). The fence alignment allows jackals free passage between two dens, and the landscape architects ensured that the resident troop of baboons could scale the fence to reach their watering hole.

The construction of roads, car-parks and picnic sites, slope stabilization and installation of ablutions and irrigation took place from 1990 to 1991. The river, which emerges from its subterranean course in the Kalahari, runs perennially and the dammed lake provides a constant source of water. From 1992 to 1993 rehabilitation of the mining area and provision of caravan and camping areas began. Currently up to 200 visitors come to the site at weekends.

Local employment was encouraged and up to 70 people were employed on the site at the peak. The works were deliberately labour intensive to promote employment, and outside contractors were required to use local labour. Site supervision was carried out by a resident landscape architect who lived on site for two years in an army tent.

The University of Witwatersrand carries out a long-term research programme in the area, currently led by Dr Jeff McKee, and fossil sites have been protected at all times. Areas of possible investigation have been determined and the future anthropological digs will be interpreted.

Proposals include the erection of an interpretation centre and restoration of the old mine buildings as reception area, tea room and crafts workshop. In early 1996 work was on hold due to lack of funds, but funding is being sought for further phases from the Southern African Development Bank and there has been an application for Unesco World Heritage Site status.

The site where the skull was found within the body of the limestone tufa.

Top: View from the tufa flow
towards the main area of
quarrying activity.

Above: Looking towards a
partially rehabilitated area
and the source of the river
emerging from the underground
Kalahari system.

Seventy local villagers were employed at the peak of the works. Here they are erecting dolerite benches carved from local Yuba River boulders at a picnic area.

Site plan

Grass

Existing vegetation

Proposed planting

Roads

Paths/tracks

Car parking

Buildings

Picnic areas

Camping

Caravaning

View points/bird hides

Distant view of a walled picnic area below cliffs with access paths made from pulverized tufa.

N

0   50 m

Boardwalks are used extensively in the park.

Water channels flow through the park.

3.7

Ibaraki Nature Park

Sugao-Numa, Iwai City, Japan

Mitsuru Man Senda, Environment Design Institute

Sugao-Numa is a 240-hectare area of marsh by the Tone River, not far from Tokyo. Ibaraki Prefecture has acquired 16 hectares of the marshland to protect it from the pressure of housing development. The Ibaraki Nature Museum has been built on an adjacent area to reveal the natural history of the site and promote its appreciation. The marsh is particularly valuable as a resting place for birds of passage. This project has certain similarities to the Parque Ecologico Xochimilco in intent (see page 95) and is not totally dissimilar from the Louisiana children's park in its position overlooking a wetland (see page 41). The main difference is the scale of this project; the museum at Ibaraki provides 12,000 square metres of floor space on three floors. The building contains exhibition rooms, a restaurant, shop, auditorium and plant research, animal research and an earth science laboratory. There is also a bird-watching café with panoramic views.

The museum lies between two hills with valley between and overlooks Sugao-Numa. On one of the hills there was a graveyard which has now been relocated. In the valley bottom old rice paddies have been converted into a pool. Most importantly, no trees were cut down to build the museum and, of course, many new trees were planted. The building is in two main sections and its bulk is broken down by its angular form: it consists of four cube forms projecting on a diagonal from a central spine which leads to a large rectangular block. The mass of the building is hidden from view of the main lake by existing woodland.

Curved paths lead down to the marshland, which is crossed by a long zig-zag causeway, and into the woodland park with its dragonfly pond and nature discovery studio.

Conservation of areas of natural interest from the pressures of urbanization requires education and the spreading of understanding. This project aims to do that and, most especially, aims to attract and inform children.

Below: The Museum building with the bird-watching café on the right-hand façade.

Bottom: Aerial view with the Nature Museum in the foreground facing the Sugao-Numa marsh with its causeway. The park is mainly to the right.

113

114

The Visitor Center seen from below the ridgeline. Felled logs were moved and stored during construction, then exactly repositioned.

The Winds of Change Trail loops through fields of blowdown logs and tree stumps. Here the process of natural regeneration can be seen all around.

Mount St Helens National Volcanic Monument

Gifford Pinchot National Forest, Washington State, USA

EDAW

On 18 May 1980 Mount St Helens erupted and changed the face of the landscape in this part of south-west Washington. The blast formed a new crater and the forests for miles around were flattened. The US Department of Agriculture's Forest Service has interpreted the volcanic eruption and its effects by means of a series of visitor centres and installations approached along a new scenic highway 504.

In 1989 the Forest Service commissioned EDAW to select sites and do the site planning and landscape design for these interpretation facilities. The first to open was the Coldwater Ridge Visitor Services Center in 1993. In 1994 there were four million visits to the National Forest, and coping with such pressures is part of the challenge of this sort of landscape design.

The Coldwater Ridge Visitor Center is on a ridge overlooking the lake and is ten kilometres from the crater. The centre has an audio-visual exhibition, catering, picnic shelters and administrative offices, and the entrance plaza is aligned on an axis with the crater and overlooks the Toutle River valley and the lake below. From the centre the Winds of Change Trail loops through fields of blowdown logs and standing tree stumps and one section of the trail cuts through the landscape to reveal a cross-section of volcanic deposition.

The Observatory on Johnston Ridge is just over 6 kilometres from the crater and looks directly into it; it has an interpretation theatre, trails, car-parking and an amphitheatre located at the edge of a precipice with views over the valley floor many hundreds of metres below. It opened in 1996.

EDAW as landscape architects were responsible for site utilization and visual analysis, and landscape and trail design. Site selection and planning are the key to the presentation of the volcano. From nearly every approach the facilities orientate the visitor to the mountain, to the consequences of the blast or other important landscape features. The landscape architects

have taken every opportunity to expose, then hide and then reveal the volcano once more.

Fundamental to the design was the requirement that everything be preserved in a natural state. The positions of felled trees were recorded so that they could be moved and stored during construction and then be repositioned exactly, almost like archaeological artefacts. Above all, this is a project that deals with ecological process and so all the new planting uses indigenous species with seed and specimens collected from the site area. In the long term the aims will be achieved by a management policy of non-interference in natural process and control of the impact of man.

The Visitor Center seen from within the car-park with Mount St Helens a looming presence.

Coldwater Ridge Visitor Services Center lies on a ridge overlooking the lake, beyond which is Mount St Helens.

Site plan:

- Vistas
- Focal points
- Mounds
- Primary footpaths
- Secondary footpaths
- New ditches/canals
- Bridges
- Existing woodland
- Proposed planting
- Avenues
- Pollarded willows
- Grass
- Boundary of country park

N

0   150 m

Natural habitat created from wasteland is what this scheme is about.

3.9
Milton Country Park
Cambridgeshire, UK

Landscape Design Associates

Milton Country Park is a large, 36-hectare park in the Cambridge Green Belt just north of the city's northern ring road, the A45. It is a fenland park, close to the River Cam, and water is its source and inspiration. The site was a mix of tips, scrapyards and car tyre dumps, with scrub and pools developed from gravel pits and former grazing land. The local authority assembled the land by compulsory purchase and the result is a piece of urban fringe remade as countryside, but supported by means of conservation and recreation rather than agriculture; and financed to a tight, local authority budget.

The design aim was to create a new landscape which appears "natural", in order to balance biodiversity and a form of landscape design on a quiet key (of course, the landscape of the fens is by its essence man-made). So the layout is an artificial creation naturalized by ecological processes which have to be actively managed to accommodate visitors and to prevent views from being overgrown or lakes from silting up.

Visitors pass through a controlled sequence of spaces, vistas and habitat types. The design ingredients are characteristic of the local fenland landscape: lines of pollarded willows and alders, grids of poplar trees, view lines along new ditches and herringbone landscape patterns, and windows cut through scrub to frame views of the lake, the bird life and the floating steel sculpture by Peter Fluck which rises from the open water of the lake.

There is a visitor centre, a 100-space car-park and six bridges, but it is the earthshaping, seeding, plantations, lake restoration and management that make the site a park and a place for fishing, for environmental education and quiet recreation. The ambition here is a form of paradise-making on an ecological basis and it represents the valuable qualities of much current English landscape architecture: quiet, unassuming, contextual and appropriate.

Windows cut through scrub to frame views of the lake.

The visitor centre designed by South Cambridgeshire District Council's Architects Department nestles in the woodland by the lake and is framed in windows cut from the lakeside vegetation. Note the wide bench which doubles as a low table.

Berjaya Langkawi Beach Resort

Burau Bay, Langkawi Islands, Malaysia

Aspinwall Clouston

Langkawi Island lies at the northern end of the Straits of Malacca on the west coast of the Malay peninsula and just south of the Thai-Malaysian border. It is a duty-free area and over a million tourists a year visit the island.

Burau Bay on Langkawi is an area of secondary tropical forest nestling into the limestone crags and foothills of the island and with a white sandy beach. The tropical forest is not strictly rainforest because there is a six-month dry season. The forest itself is fairly open and this eased access; it is secondary forest having already been logged. The main tree species were either the climax forest trees, which are predominantly *Dipterocarpus sp.*, or coastal trees such as *Eugenia* and sea hibiscus.

The Beach Resort consists of a 394-room hotel largely made up of small kampong-style buildings or guest houses/bedrooms and a larger central facility with staff quarters and plant nursery attached. Most of the guest houses are located within the forest, though some areas are in more open lawns planted with new trees. Twenty-one of the total 28 hectares are forest and this is a relatively low-density development for such a large hotel.

The positions of the existing trees largely dictated the layout. Roads were set out on site by eye, jointly by the resident landscape architect, the contractor's supervisor and the machine driver. No trees over 30 centimetres in diameter were felled. The siting of buildings was done by pegging them out on the ground to ensure they fitted the lie of the land and the forest. Similarly, the locating of the main building platforms was done jointly by landscape architect and architect in order to avoid major earthworks.

Landscape came first: the main building is on the right.

Plan: This is a large, 394-bed hotel resort. The larger hotel facilities are grouped in the main building (for example, ballroom, conference suite, theme pub, restaurant and reception), overlooking the swimming pool and sea. The staff quarters and nursery are to the right. The guest houses are tucked into the forest. No trees over 30 centimetres in diameter were felled, and the existing forest, mangrove swamp (off plan, bottom right) and landform dictated the layout.

The existing mangrove swamp below the central hotel facility was totally protected: the contractor was not allowed to approach it, and siltation controls were used to avoid spillage. The larger hotel facilities, with ballroom, conference suite, theme pub and restaurant, are located in a rather grand building which, together with the nearby staff quarters, was sited on land that had been previously cleared for a rubber plantation. Below the central facilities is a swimming pool made of concrete with natural features on three sides: bamboo groves, the mangrove swamp and a tree-lined stream. The pool was also laid out to fit the existing ground. The lie of the land allowed the construction of an artificial rock face of glass reinforced plastic based on moulds taken from nearby natural rock formations, and now a waterfall cascades into the swimming pool.

Paths and roads are in brushed concrete over which forest debris and grit is allowed to fall; Kempas hardwood timber is used for boardwalks, bridges, shelters, signs and lampposts. The buildings are concrete framed, faced in timber and roofed with local terracotta tiles.

The whole idea was to allow the hotel to be dominated by the existing forest and land form and not to sacrifice environmental quality to functional convenience. Guest rooms are often accessed by steep paths; restaurants might be half a kilometre from a guest room; the climate is hot and there are numerous insects in the forest. This may seem like a recipe for commercial disaster, but the guests love the experience and it is the forest rooms that are the most popular.

Opposite: The artificial rock in g.r.p. (glass reinforced plastic), waterfall and swimming pool below the main building. The rockwork is based on moulds of local rock faces.

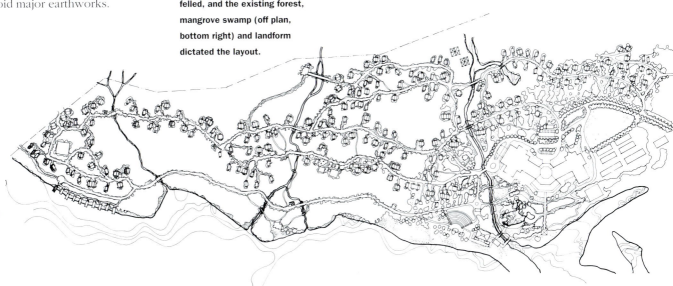

120

Chuo Plaza in Momochi
Seaside Park, Fukuoka City,
Japan (see page 133). Zen's
design for this park bridges the
coastal highway and joins
together the town and the
beach beyond.

4 Urban Design & Housing

Pershing Square

Los Angeles, California, USA

Ricardo Legorreta and Hanna/Olin

Pershing Square dates from 1866 and has been redesigned several times. It was named after General Pershing in 1918, and in the 1950s a 1,800-space, underground car-park was built beneath it. By the 1980s it was rundown, a place for the homeless and for drug pushers.

It is located in downtown Los Angeles between Fifth Street and Sixth Street. As with Bryant Park in New York (also redesigned by Hanna/Olin), it was adjacent property owners who led the campaign to revitalize Pershing Park. The result is a radical rethink and transformation as a joint effort by the Pershing Square Property Owners Association and the city's Community Redevelopment Agency. The Los Angeles City Department of Recreation and Parks maintains the park.

In 1991 SITE Projects of New York won the open competition to redesign the park, but its proposal was thought to be too expensive. So the redesign was awarded to Hanna/Olin and Ricardo Legorreta who had both worked with Maguire Thomas Partners previously. It was Maguire Thomas who acted as catalyst by investing an initial $1.5 million of seed monies. Ultimately the 18-member Pershing Property Owners Association raised $8.5 million through voluntary tax assessments and $6 million was contributed by the Community Regeneration Authority. The Regeneration Authority works with social agencies to offer counselling and care to the homeless attracted to the square.

The collaboration between Ricardo Legorreta, based in Mexico City, and Laurie Olin, based in Philadelphia, has transformed the square.

The design is organized orthogonally and follows the city grid. Rising from the pink concrete paving is a ten-storey, purple rendered bell tower, and an attached aqueduct wall also in purple. There are square windows in this wall which frame views from the square to smaller garden areas.

On the other side of the square is a canary-yellow café and a triangular transit stop or bus station which back on to another purple wall. Along each street front are the existing ramps to the underground garage, and a continuous sidewalk has been added to cut across the access to these ramps. Effectively there are four main entrances to the square, sited at the four corners.

The edges of the square are defined by groups of trees in rows of two or three. The groups or bosques,

Ranks of ruddy-pink columns. The use of colour is bright and provocative.

Opposite: Pershing Square is in the heart of downtown Los Angeles and much of the money for its revitalization came from adjacent property owners who wished to upgrade the square to protect their property values.

when they have established, will hide the impact of the roads around the square while maintaining the links with the surrounding bowl of buildings. On the east side, fronting Hill Street, 48 tall palm trees from the old park have been transplanted to form a great palm court beside the bell tower. The palms are interspersed with existing statues and features and one of Legoretta's characteristic terracotta balls.

In the centre of the square is a grove of orange trees (*Citrus sp.*), so characteristic of Los Angeles, and other trees include bird of paradise (*Strelitzia*), date palm (*Phoenix dactylifera*) and Mexican fan palm (*Washingtonia robusta*), yucca, camphor (*Cinnamomum*), sweet gum (*Eucalyptus*), *Tipuana* and *Ficus*.

A circular water basin and sunken square amphitheatre provide two elements of regular geometry in the park. The basin is paved to form a great, dished circle of grey pebbles which lie flush with the surrounding paving. At the edges, water from the aqueduct wall falls into the centre of the pool and the water rises and falls in tidal fashion on an eight-minute cycle. A jagged shape representing an earthquake fissure emerges from the centre of the pool.

The 2,000-capacity amphitheatre is grassed and stepped in the pink concrete. The stage is marked by four Canary Island Palm trees (*Phoenix canariensis*) and, like the water, it is arranged symmetrically. The whole design of the square is distinctive for its use of formal plan symmetry which is offset by a balanced asymmetry of vertical elements such as the tower, the walls and the café.

Pershing Square is not fenced, but it is intensively managed and it opens from 5.30 a.m. to 10.30 p.m. The Pershing Square café is run by the Biltmore Hotel and there is a programme of cultural activities in the park. This is an ambitious effort in the revitalization of central city space and is part of a wider programme of property improvements linked with social improvement. As a design this is a plaza in the Mediterranean or Latin tradition and it aims to serve the different communities of Los Angeles that meet here.

The purple bell tower is rectangular in plan and, except for a great wedge shape which rises the full height on the inner side of the tower, is simple and unadorned. From the junction of tower and wedge runs a purple aqueduct which leads to a circular basin where the water rises and falls like a tide on an eight-minute cycle.

The earthquake line, designed by artist Barbara McCarren, runs from the circular basin across the square in the direction of the corner of Sixth Street and Olive Street. It is created out of black terrazzo in the centre, edged with golden and charcoal-grey quartzite slabs.

Site plan

In the pool by the restaurant a
curve is introduced to follow
the line of the building.
Patterns are made with moving
water.

4.2
Iki-Iki Plaza
12 Ichiban-cho, Chiyoda-ku, Tokyo, Japan

Shodo Suzuki

This is an example of making the most out of a very limited area. Around Chiyoda Ward Municipal Hall (which contains a swimming pool and an old people's welfare institute) Shodo Suzuki has carved out a garden space in granite and ironstone from the wasteland of narrow areas left over from the building development.

The north-facing entrance front consists of granite slabs laid in lines symmetrically angled to centre on the main axis of the building. On the west is a narrow garden space overlooked by offices and a restaurant where there is another linear composition in stone, but here the lines are parallel with the building. A water channel runs alongside the building and flows into a pool curved to repeat the line of the restaurant, which protrudes from the south-western corner of the building. The pool is patterned at regular intervals with bubble fountains which create concentric circles of ripples; the pool catches the sun and reflects the ripples into the restaurant. Slabs of granite with some faces rough and some smooth rise from the stone floor to form sculptural seats and basins. This garden is a composition of stone, partially cut smooth and partially left rough.

On the south side a perimeter wall forms a backdrop to a waterfall which faces the lobby of the main auditorium. Beside the waterfall is a small Japanese-style garden which is overlooked by a conference room.

The waterfall, made from a recomposed Chinese quarry face, makes a sombre and exceptionally strong visual impact.

127

The rock waterfall is a *tour de force*. It was created by identifying a section of granite quarry face in China that "was full of character and expression". The design was then governed by the size and weight of the pieces of stone that could be transported; this determined how the quarry stone could be cut. A mock-up was made in the quarry, which was then recorded and each stone identified; Shodo Suzuki explains that "the shape of the 'stone scene' was drawn on the raw ore using indian ink".

Then came the challenge of re-erecting the stones on the restricted site in Tokyo. Once the rock face had been put together, it was necessary to adjust it to allow for the flow of the water. The result is a natural rock face changed by cutting and manipulation to produce, not an exact re-creation, but rather a reshaping consequent on the interplay of cutting, water flow and appropriateness to the new site.

This is an example of a public landscape created using techniques and sensibilities typical of Japanese private garden-making. New spaces have been created seemingly out of nowhere and wasteland has been transformed into a series of public spaces.

The water channel in granite: in these narrow shady spaces it is important to capture light and movement by the use of water.

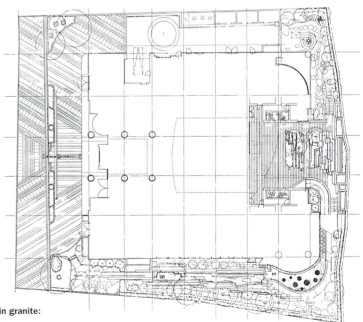

Plan showing the narrowness of the spaces with which Shodo Suzuki had to work.

Drainage grating set in grey gneiss slabs.

Trees are protected by decorative iron grilles.

Ole Bulls Plass

Bergen, Norway

Arkitektgruppen Cubus

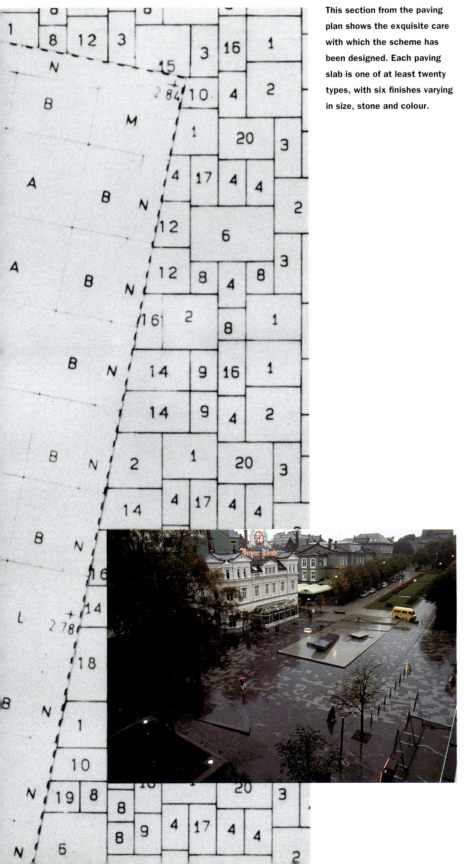

This section from the paving plan shows the exquisite care with which the scheme has been designed. Each paving slab is one of at least twenty types, with six finishes varying in size, stone and colour.

This plaza is part of Bergen's policy since 1989 of reducing traffic in the city centre and giving priority to public transport and the pedestrian. Initially Cubus was commissioned to masterplan the traffic calming; design competitions followed for some 14 streets and a square, and Cubus began its design work for Ole Bulls Plass in 1992.

Originally, Ole Bulls Plass was a traditional park of birch trees, rockeries and a statue of the violinist Ole Bull. It lies next to the main city square, Torgalmenningen. In 1986 Sveinung Skjold redesigned the park in a Japanese style. Now it has been completely transformed in a collaboration between the landscape architects of Cubus, Ingrid Haukeland and Arne Sœlen, and sculptor Asbjörn Andresen as part of the city-centre traffic calming. It has become a traffic-free square serving the restaurants, hotels, department stores and theatres of the area.

The ground has been transformed into a carpet of granite and gneiss open to all and focused on Andresen's Blue Slab sculpture in Brazilian sodalite. Though car-free, the square has been designed to take service traffic, and the paving is laid on a concrete foundation. The paving consists of 4,000 slabs of predominately grey gneiss and granite with increasing use of pink granite towards the corners. There are six different finishes to the paving stones, and this is a place intended to be seen in the rain. Bergen is a very rainy city, with a rainfall of 2,500 millimetres per annum, and so the square is drained by two 80-metre long monsoon drains. The paving stones when wet reveal their colour, texture and pattern and reflect the life around. The whole is an exercise in exquisite minimalism, exploiting subtle variations in the stone, as if it were a tactile and environmental painting with geology.

A high-level view of the plaza reveals a symphony in stone. In the centre is Asbjörn Andresen's Blue Slab in sodalite surrounded by the rhythm of grey gneiss paving slabs giving way to predominantly pink granite towards the edges of the space.

Vichy main post office fronts on to a rectangular white plain of marble crazy paving (on the right). This orthogonal frame is counterpoised by the ship-like lozenge shapes planted with trees, the great pool and the diagonal in grey stone which connects the place to the square lawn on the left.

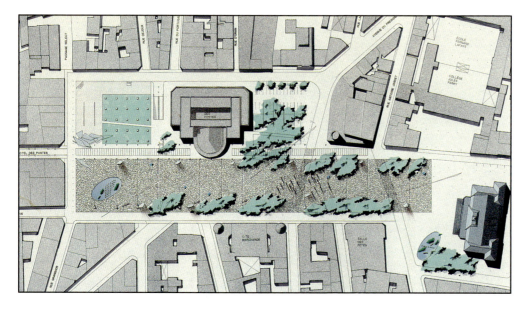

Site plan

4.4
Place Charles de Gaulle
Vichy, France

Latitude Nord

Set in front of the Vichy main post office, this is a major new forum for the town at the meeting point of the main shopping streets and halfway between the railway station and the spa establishment. The design consists of a new long, rectangular *place* in a great white plain of marble crazy paving like broken sea ice, marked by small, irregularly set triangles and squares of dark stone. Sailing through the sea of ice are angular ship-like beds planted with low bamboo and trees like masts. The whole square is enclosed with a band of dark paving, patterned with regular dashed lines of white stone. Along the street frontage walls in the form of arrowheads rise as if to repel cars, and the cafés across the street spread their tables in the square. The whole *place* tilts slightly towards a blue, ceramic-lined, lozenge-shaped pool with spray fountains.

Set on diagonal axes away from the main square and to either side of the town hall there are subsidiary spaces. One (where a car ramp leads down to an underground car-park) is mainly filled with a square lawn cut in two by a pointed diagonal in dark grey stone. Beyond the lawn is a construction of white stone pillars illuminated at night and supporting wired wisteria and also summertime tent structures to shade café tables. The space on the other side of the town hall is more vegetated: the ship-like shapes planted with trees in the main square congregate here more closely.

Gilles Vexlard and Laurence Vacherot of Latitude Nord are working in a land where mayors have powers of public patronage and the appearance and form of public spaces in a town are seen as expressions of civic worth. They are from the Versailles Landscape School and can be seen as followers of the school of Jacques Simon. The Place Charles de Gaulle is in the tradition of strong formal expression of a design. There is a restrained use of colour which is confined to the one great gesture in ultramarine in the pool. The *place* is made special by the use of line to describe and fit with the surrounding buildings. The great plain that is the white marble *place* resonates like a musical instrument, partially through visual features such as the use of the points of small dark stone and partially through the social interplay of the citizens of Vichy who here are set on a very public stage.

The edge of the pool: the diffuse spray from the fountains (off-picture to the left) produce a dappled, lapping water surface which is translated to a smooth overflow by the recessed edge.

Café tables and the arrowhead walls define the street edge of the square along the Rue du Paradis. The blue pool is animated with spray fountains in its centre.

Looking landward at night along the western axis with the rows of bubble fountains set between an avenue of multi-stemmed trees. Note the Japanese appreciation of the moon above: moongazing and nocturnal views are often forgotten in European landscape design.

Chuo Plaza in Momochi Seaside Park

Fukuoka City, Japan

Zen Environmental Design

This plaza forms a promenade within Momochi Seaside Park, but it is a seaside promenade with a major distinguishing difference: it is elevated over a major road and car-park. The approach on the landward side is stepped up to bridge the road and leads to the plaza with its views over Hakata Bay on the north side of Japan's southernmost island, Kyushu.

On the landward side the plaza faces and is overlooked by the Fukuoka Tower, and as you walk to the steps leading up to the plaza you glimpse the tops of the seven light pillars above. The steps wrap around and up to a U-shaped central bay with a small pool and a glistening granite globe washed by water. A water channel leads to a small pyramid set in a raised pool and also washed by water emerging from its top. Here you choose to either move west to an urban area in crazy paving or east to a more gardenesque area. The western axis leads along an avenue of multi-stemmed trees marked by underlit bubble fountains, and lined on one side by seats recessed into the rendered wall. This axis ends in a circular walled rest space. The eastward route leads along a line of light columns and past the gardenesque shrub and tree area. The western and eastern axes come together again at the seaside edge. Here you can descend to the beach by symmetrical steps which become almost baroque in their curves.

This plaza is an exercise in symmetry and asymmetry, a composition of many small and quiet touches put together in a way that maintains a strong coherence. It is a place to meet, a place to view the sea and the setting sun or gaze at the moon.

High-level view of the plaza showing the main coastal road in cutting and the outlook over Hakata Bay.

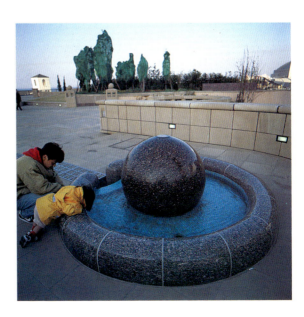

The granite globe fountain in the bay at the head of the steps on the landward side. The trees in the distance are wrapped for protection against sea winds.

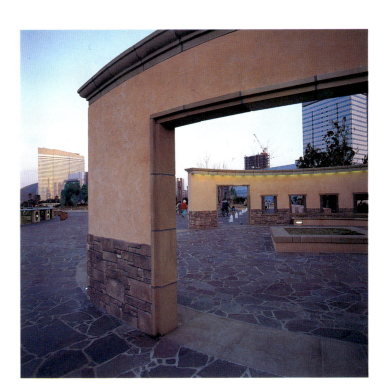

Right: The circular rest space at dusk with the western axis of bubble fountains framed in the distance and the area set in a sea of crazy-paving stones in Italian porphyry.

Left: The row of seven light columns establishes the eastward axis; they lead from the sea approach to the pyramid fountain. Note how the lines of the Australian sandstone paving are crossed by the linear pattern of columnar tree shadows.

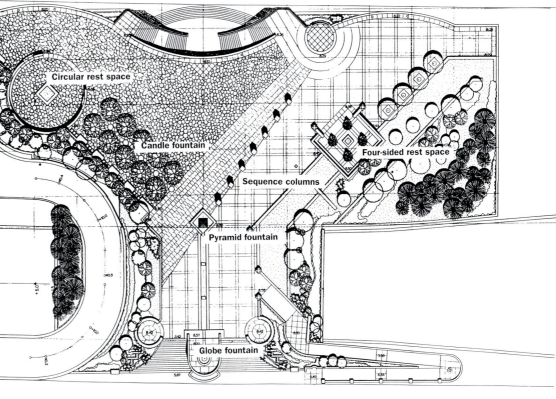

Site plan showing the sunken highway on both sides of the plaza.

The Belvedere

Battery Park City, New York, USA

Child Associates

The Belvedere site is the last link in the 2.5 kilometre chain of waterfront spaces and parks facing the Hudson River in Lower Manhattan. All have been created on landfill since the early 1980s in connection with the development of the new, 235-hectare commercial and residential Battery Park City on the site of the old piers off West Street. The Belvedere is at the pivot of the waterfront where the Trans-Hudson ferry lands, just north of North Cove Yacht Harbor and overlooked by the World Financial Center building.

The park consists of a raised platform planted with regular rows of English oak trees (*Quercus robur*). An esplanade runs along the water's edge and turns at a right angle into the Yacht Harbor and towards the World Financial Center and the Winter Gardens. At the angle itself is the circular Belvedere, edged in a ring of Dakota mahogany granite paving. From here there are views across the Hudson River to New Jersey and the Statue of Liberty. The Belvedere is planted with honey locusts (*Gleditsia triacanthos*). Between the upper area bosque area, paved in terracotta stone dust, and the esplanade is a grand sloped wall of rusticated, grey Dakota mahogany granite which sinuously meanders in great curves

along the river frontage. It is not very high, just over a metre, but the batter and the rustication give it a strong presence and it has a wide coping. Set well back on the coping is a smooth round teak rail which forms a backrest for those sitting along the wall to watch the sun set over the Hudson. Long curved steps provide a link between the esplanade and the upper area.

At the water's edge, 25-metre wide steps lead to the river, and the ends of the steps are marked by two tall, stainless steel pylons by the sculptor Martin Puryear. One is a spiral, the other a series of solid wedges and they serve as a welcome to ferry travellers. The spiral is lit from within, while the wedges, are underlit, and black, traditional-style lampposts line the river's edge. Underneath the park there is a plethora of underground services, and rather curiously it is claimed as a virtue that the surface water drainage runs into the Manhattan sewers rather than into the river.

This is a remarkably simple space, beautifully detailed and well proportioned: it is a small gesture which becomes a big welcome.

The view from the Belvedere of the River Hudson under the foliage of honey locust (*Gleditsia triacanthos*).

Opposite: The two pylons by sculptor Martin Puryear act as counterpoints to the Statue of Liberty in New York Harbor and as markers for those arriving by the Trans-Hudson ferry. This scheme is all about views, identity and landmarks.

Sketch: bird's-eye view

1 To North Park
2 Esplanade
3 Ferry terminal
4 Belvedere
5 Bosquet

140

The view from North Cove Yacht Harbor of the riverside walk: the Belvedere is at the angle where the walk turns from the Yacht Harbor to run along the River Hudson and link with Hudson River Park.

The sloped and slightly rusticated wall. The steps double as seating and the teak rail serves as a backrest.

The high-rise of Battery Park
City towers above the
Belvedere steps; the arched
structure is the Winter
Gardens.

Plan: the straight line at the
river's edge is counterpoised
by the sinuous curves of the
sloping walls, and the circular
belvedere turns the scheme
towards the Yacht Harbor to
the right.

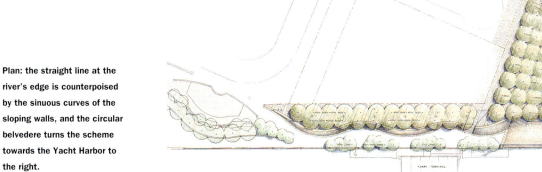

N

142

The area between the
apartment blocks: the
colonnades provide shelter in
heavy rain. The standard of
provision of landscape is
remarkable given that this
is social housing.

4.8
Ma Hang Village

Stanley, Hong Kong

Landscape Group, Hong Kong Housing Authority

In China, including Hong Kong, interest in rockeries and traditional garden forms continues and they are applied to non-traditional situations such as high-rise housing estates. Ma Hang is a valley near Stanley on the south side of Hong Kong island. Six thousand villagers who were squatting in the valley have now been rehoused by the Hong Kong Housing Authority in a new village consisting of six ten-storey high apartment blocks (this is relatively low-rise for Hong Kong). These standard, system-built blocks are grouped around a central landscape spine that consists of a stream system with pools. Roads providing emergency and service access penetrate only as far as the outside of each apartment block, and the central landscape spine is traffic-free and interlaced with footpaths. Parking is underground in a two-level car-park which takes advantage of the fall of the land and is covered with vegetation.

The system-built housing blocks have been sited to follow the topography – the site has not been levelled – and they are painted in bands of colour ranging from a lime green near the ground to reddish browns at the tops in variously three or five layers. The roofs are tiled and the grouping can be easily viewed from the higher slope above.

Existing trees have been retained and the flow of the existing stream used for the new series of water features that provides the focus for the development. It is necessary to design for typhoons and monsoons in Hong Kong. Use is intense, so materials are designed to be hard-wearing: in situ concrete paths with edges of granite setts. There are versions of chinoiserie-style concrete structures, and glazed tile roofs are used for shelters and walkways. Granite steps have been used but most of the rockwork by the waterside and under the shade of buildings is artificial, using glass fibre reinforced concrete. The designers have aimed to create the effects of the small natural streams which cut deep into the soft granite slopes on the southern side of Hong Kong island until they meet the harder underlying rock. Where the water is quick-moving a stratified and craggy rock has been simulated which is heavily fissured, especially in the main waterfall. The rockwork has also been "wrapped around" the water at the main waterfall to prevent wind blow in what is an exposed area. Where the water is gentler the artificial rock is much smoother with a shingle trim, and there are large rounded boulders placed

A waterfall in artificial rock. Note the heavily fissured rock effect and the way the rocks wrap around the water.

as if they had been brought down by some heavy torrent.

High-rise social housing is a worldwide challenge for landscape architects, and designs often have not survived intense use and lack of care and maintenance. The example of the Hong Kong Housing Authority is inspiring, both in terms of using a traditional and popular design style and as an example of provision of social public space for mass housing.

Site plan

CAPE ROAD EXTENSION

146

The west end of the lake from
the bridge; to the left are the
large, three-storey high
Liquidamber styraciflua shortly
after planting in 1995. The
pebbles hide the plastic liner
in the lake.

A steel gazebo that will soon
be festooned with *Wisteria
sinensis*.

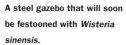

The mall on the south side of
the lake planted with trees and
with the four steel gazebos
projecting diagonally into
the lake.

148

**Plan with trees and the
underground Rotterdam Blaak
station to the right.**

**The Binnenrotte with
Laurenskerk church to the
right.**

Binnenrotte Market Square

Rotterdam, The Netherlands

West 8 Landscape Architects

The overhead railway running through this part of central Rotterdam has been rebuilt underground, allowing the creation of a vast new market place. The scheme, by Rotterdam-based landscape architects West 8, pulls together fragments of the old city centre destroyed by German bombs in 1940. These fragments included the dam or bund of the filled-in River Rotte, the Laurenskerk church, the statue of Erasmus and evidence of the blitzkrieg.

The design is a vast void or field in the middle of the city which becomes a space of opportunity for habitation, especially so when it fills with up to 70,000 people in the twice-weekly markets where the Rotterdamers buy their second-hand furniture, cheap stockings and trainers and eat the eel, soused herring or chips and mayonnaise at foodstalls.

When empty the space is a challenging void. It is paved in oversized 11 x 33-centimetre, grey concrete blocks laid on a 3 over 4 staggered running bond in vertical strips which accentuate the vastness of this 4.5-hectare square. Around the space is a border of 17-centimetre high, black plinths with a huge 60-centimetre kerb and a neat anti-parking tubular rail that can recess into the paving under two galvanized steel plates on market days to allow lorry and trailer access. The genius of this square is in its challenging functionalism – there is no pussy-footing prettiness here. It is simple, it is big, it works and shows sophistication in the appropriate and hugely tough detailing: a huge blue steel cage or Fietspen for bicycles (*fiets* means bike), litter bins, *Robinia* timber benches, mast lights and just a few untrimmed plane trees (*Platanus acerifolia*). There is a small red cabin for the market inspectors. Electricity points supply the market trader and clamps secure the overhead cables on market days.

This scheme is quintessential Rotterdam: straight, tough, honest functionalism and as typically and thoroughly Dutch as a tugboat, a pair of clogs or a Rietveld house.

Vast and functional: the Binnenrotte is exquisitely detailed as in this anchor point.

This is a space to be lived in, a place with a whole range of opportunities for city life.

Anti-vehicle bars can be recessed into the paving to allow entry for market vehicles.

150

Place de la République: the
fountain jets are set at a low
and oblique angle to wash the
square.

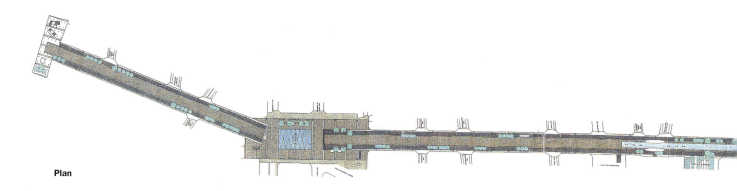

Plan

Rue de la République

Lyons, France

Alain Sarfati – AREA

The Moroccan-born, Paris-based architect and *urbaniste* Alain Sarfati is perhaps best known for his public housing (as at Cergy-Pontoise – Les Egvérets) and his exciting computer graphics. His urbanistic work has included the landscape planning of the RN7 highway along the Riviera.

Lyons is chief among the many French cities and towns which have been improving their public spaces, squares, parks and streets since the 1970s. Alain Sarfati's work in Lyons has included the pedestrianization link to the new Lyons metro. The 1.2-kilometre long, 22-metre wide Rue de la République is in the centre of the city, north-south and parallel with the two rivers, the Rhône and the Saône. It runs from the Hôtel de Ville in the north, through a series of squares which each connect with bridges crossing the rivers, and terminates in the Rue de la Barre in the south.

Sarfati considers Lyons to be part of the Mediterranean in terms of culture, light, sun forms and shadows, and he has used this inspiration of Mediterranean life and light to inspire his urban design work. The repaved street is in granite: white granite from Berrocal and blue from Lanhein. It runs straight from the Hôtel de Ville to the Place de la République, which acts as a rectangular pivot for a slight turn of angle west for the remainder of the street.

The Place de la République is marked by a great fountain set piece. A series of jet fountains are arranged in two rows on either side of a central basin. The fountains shoot inwards in great oblique arcs which meet near the centre of the *place*. The basin itself is delineated like a swimming pool by lanes marked in the darker stone. This theme of delineation carries through the whole street in a unity of colour, material and treatment. Sarfati sums up the project as a metaphor: "*Mare Noestrum devient un projet*" (The Mediterranean [literally "our sea"] becomes the project).

The jet fountain backlit at night.

The granite detailing is hard and robust, yet rather elegant.

Trees grow out of the rock.

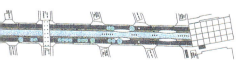

152

Forum Bonn office building, Germany (see page 171). View of the moat surrounding the pyramid, with the stone pergola to the left, covered in *Wisteria sinensis*. The main entrance to the building can be seen in the background.

5 Offices & Institutions

Redwood trees in the Grove
with swirling mist.

5.1

Prospect Green

Rancho Cordova, Sacramento Valley, California, USA

Hargreaves Associates

Set in a landscape reclaimed from hydraulic dredge mining in the 1850s, Prospect Park is a 13-hectare office park with a proposed 50,000 square metres of offices. George Hargreaves has designed a masterplan which concentrates lush, park-like landscape effects in a central, crescent-shaped, 1.2-hectare campus which has been created prior to the construction of the buildings; the landscape design came first.

Around the central crescent is a tree-lined promenade that will link future buildings. The crescent is bisected by a walkway and the two halves are designed differently. The western half is open lawn enclosed by the promenade of trees. The eastern half consists of the Grove and the Garden. The Grove is an outdoor room, 30 metres in diameter. Within it is a double ring of 16 redwoods (*Sequoia sempervirens*), each planted more than 10 metres high. The redwoods enclose and shade a sunken bowl of grass, depressed just over a metre below the surrounding levels. At the centre of the grove is a circular concrete terrace with nozzles that emit clouds of mist. This lowers the temperature by 10 degrees Fahrenheit and creates a cool, outdoor space in the hot Sacramento sun. The mist operates in cycles at 10 a.m., 12 to 2 p.m. and again at 3 p.m. The mist is lit from below at night and plays tricks with the sunlight during the day – as it responds to subtle changes in the breeze and in humidity, it gathers, hangs about and disappears at intervals. During one cycle it emanates from the centre of the plaza; at other times it creates a ring around it. Round glass covers contain the mist nozzles and rest over uplights. Light and mist share the same point of origin and create dramatic effects at night.

To the east of the Grove the ground becomes a series of intertwined landforms symbolic of the tailings and deep cuts left after dredge mining. These landforms divide the area into secluded valleys; they are shaded by small trees and furnished with stone seats carved from local Yuba River boulders, saw cut to carve the seats and reveal the inner pattern of the stone. Each boulder weighs up to 250 kilogrammes. The steep sides of the landforms are planted with low-maintenance, drought-tolerant strawberry clover (*Trifolium fragiferum*) on the longer sides and with dwarf bamboo and day lilies (*Hemerocallis sp.*) on the triangular "cut" ends.

The mist emitters in the Grove are set in glass mounts that are underlit: this is landscape architecture as theatre set.

The water-use strategy for the park concentrates the lawn and redwoods in the central depressed area where they benefit from run-off and the mist fountains. As the land rises, more upland species of trees are used and the grass lawn is reduced to narrow path side strips beyond which drought-tolerant clover and wild flowers are used.

The design provides a communal, outdoor room for the office workers: the landscape area in the office park has been concentrated to form a usable community amenity rather than being dispersed in small, show-off strips in front of each development parcel. The Grove with its amphitheatre-like space provides a place for lunch-time concerts and evening gatherings. The Green with its shaded walk can accommodate a street fair or a festival. This is landscape design taking hold of a commercial office park development and giving it a true community campus.

To the east of the Grove the ground becomes a series of intertwined landforms symbolic of the tailings and deep cuts left after dredge mining.

Below the trees there are long beds of low ferns under the hornbeam, and periwinkle (*Vinca minor*) under the limes with, at intervals, bronze cat benches designed by Judy McKee.

The courtyard is set between a nineteenth-century shopfront facing the Avenue Montaigne and a modern office block that backs on to the Impasse d'Antin.

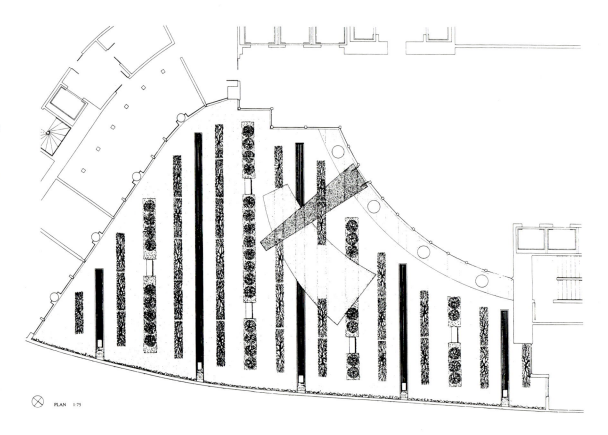

PLAN 1:75

50 Avenue Montaigne Courtyard

Paris, France

Michael Van Valkenburgh Associates

This courtyard scheme in central Paris is set between a nineteenth-century shopfront facing the Avenue Montaigne and a modern office block which backs on to the Impasse d'Antin. Underneath is a subterranean car-park. The courtyard is a private place where employees can relax.

The American landscape architect Michael Van Valkenburgh has placed lines of long water channels across the courtyard which end in thin, 6-metre high tubular columns covered in stretched translucent stainless-steel fabric: water drips from the top of the steel columns, which are underlit. Between the water channels are rows of trees. The trees are either lines of lime (*Tilia euchlora*), trained as espaliers to make living curtains, or rows of fastigiate hornbeam (*Carpinus betulus fastigiata*). Below the trees are long beds of low ferns under the hornbeam and periwinkle (*Vinca minor*) under the limes. At intervals there are benches in the form of sculptural, flat-backed bronze cats, designed by Judy McKee.

The glass lobby of the building has a clear view of the courtyard within and the entrance is marked by a slash of raised, chequerboard steel plate which is at the level of the lobby. It cuts across a raised platform of stainless steel, and the whole garden is slightly sunken to give a feeling of permanence and solidity. The rear wall of the courtyard is clothed in ivy (*Hedera helix baltica*).

This is an example of design making order out of disorder. Previously, the buildings protruded chaotically and the space made no sense. Van Valkenburgh has imposed a linear order which composes the space. Indeed the interior designers for the office building, Kohn Pederson Fox, have continued this linear theme in their design for the lobby.

Michael Van Valkenburgh's designs reflect his interests in the geometry of seventeenth-century French gardens such as Le Nôtre's gardens at Sceaux and Courances and the work of Jean de la Quintine. His achievement in the Avenue Montaigne has been to take this historical tradition and renew it, giving the ideas contemporary relevance and life in a way that creates spaces of sounds, smells and tactile qualities which are also stages for contemporary social theatre. This is an austere and restrained, yet very appropriate, approach to landscape design.

A slash of chequerboard steel plate cuts across a raised platform of stainless steel and contrasts with the regular lines of trees and water channels.

Van Valkenburgh has placed lines of long water channels across the courtyard with rows of trees between the channels, either lime (*Tilia euchlora*) trained as espaliers or rows of fastigiate hornbeam (*Carpinus betulus fastigiata*).

Detail of the raised, chequerboard steel plate meeting the platform of stainless steel.

Aerial view of the entry court:
an exercise in regular
geometry.

Plaza Tower

South Coast Plaza, Costa Mesa, California, USA

Peter Walker, William Johnson and Partners

South Coast Plaza Town Center in Orange County has been developed over the past 25 years. Peter Walker first began work here in the early 1970s while still at Sasaki Walker Associates, when he and his SWA colleagues designed the 5-hectare Town Center Park in a curvilinear, almost Olmstedian tradition. Since then a series of commercial and cultural buildings has been constructed around the park extending to 15 hectares, and Walker has constantly updated the masterplan and designed the landscape of individual buildings.

Plaza Tower is one of the more recent developments. It is a joint venture by the Segerstrom family and IBM and serves as IBM's regional headquarters. Cesar Pelli designed a corporate palazzo in stainless steel which contrasts with the stone cladding of the other office buildings, and so Walker chose to apply steel to the site landscape.

Stainless steel is not so usual in landscape design, but it works in southern California: it catches and reflects the atmosphere, light and clarity of Orange County, changing from a shimmer in bright sunlight, to glowing oranges and reds at sunset to steely grey on overcast mornings.

Walker has laid 100-millimetre wide bands of steel across the entry court paving connecting the Plaza Tower to a multi-storey car-park; rings of stainless steel form pools and weirs on both sides of the entrance and steel light bollards mark the approaches. These bands, circles and bollard colonnades cross and overlap to create a geometrical composition whether viewed from above or on the ground; indeed the reflecting pools grab the elevation of the Tower and project it downwards, creating a double geometry. This is corporate America made art and made urbane.

The steel-edged pool reflects the steel façade of the building.

The rigorous discipline of Cesar Pelli's stainless steel building elevation is translated and reflected in Peter Walker's landscape design.

The view from the Tower across the entry court with the car-park building beyond.

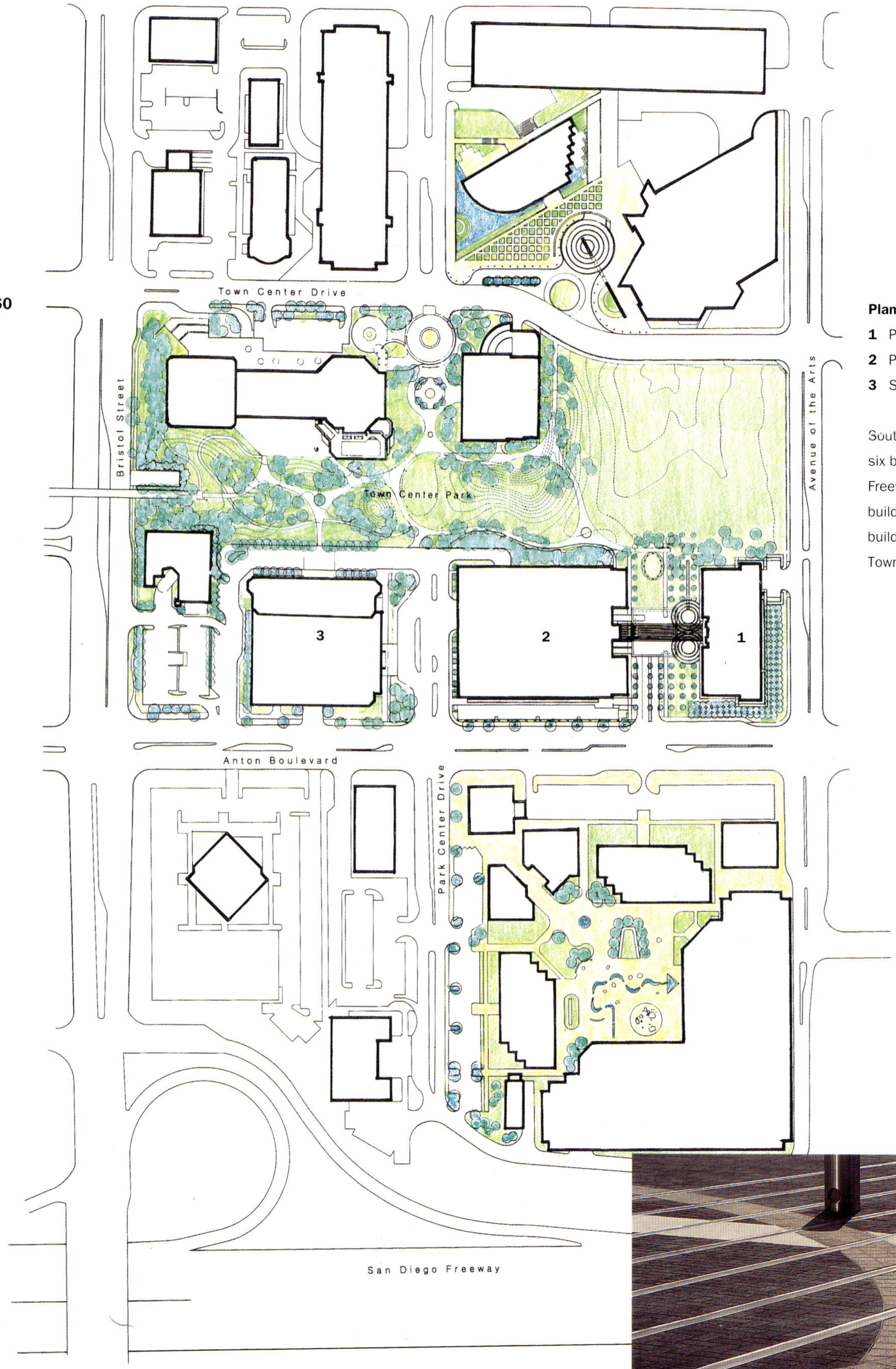

Plan

1 Plaza Tower

2 Parking structure

3 South Coast Plaza Hotel

South Plaza Town Center covers six blocks off the San Diego Freeway and consists of cultural buildings, offices and car-park buildings grouped around the Town Center Park.

Town Center Drive

Bristol Street

Town Center Park

Avenue of the Arts

3

2

1

Anton Boulevard

Park Center Drive

San Diego Freeway

The simple ingredients of the scheme include grey and light-buff paviors across which have been laid 100-millimetre wide bands of stainless steel.

Rings of steel hold circles
of water, grass and paving:
function and geometry combine
in the entry court to create a
sense of arrival.

162

Detail of the foot of the moss mountain (to the left) with finely raked gravel and stepping stones.

Centre for Advanced Science and Technology

Harima Science Garden City, Hyogo Prefecture, Japan

Peter Walker, William Johnson and Partners

Peter Walker is the landscape architect for the new 2,000-hectare science city project set in the mountains west of Kyoto. This high technology centre is a conference facility to house visitors and provide a resource for smaller R. & D. companies. The buildings were designed by Arata Isozaki, with whom Peter Walker also collaborated on the science city masterplan.

The visitor enters a car-park made into a garden by surrounding hedges of evergreen oak (*Quercus glauca*) with a central grid of grassed volcanic cones each surmounted by a juniper (*Juniperus virginiana* "Skyrocket") with a red light on top. These volcanic forms remind us of the origins of the mountains around the site. The Walker signature of mist spray (which was used in his scheme for Harvard Yard, Cambridge, Massachusetts nearly 20 years ago) is all about.

Within the building a courtyard features a mountain of squared stone rip rap curving upwards and an equally large moss mountain. Diagonal paths of stepping-stone slabs and timber planks lead to the

Between the two mountains, stone and moss, runs a straight line of stepping stones.

buildings over gravel sharply raked to follow the curves of the conic mountains. Framing these features is a regularly planted grove of bamboo that gives forth mist spray and dampens the moss. In the evening, lights project silhouettes of small trees on to the walls, so making the "mountains" seem immense. This is a viewing garden to be seen from the entrance area and the conference facilities.

There is also a Director's garden with lawn and gravel paths shaded by a grove of conifers. Laid across both gravel and grass is a grid of small circular pools flush with the ground, and at night these glow and light up the underside of the trees.

In this design, Walker reinterprets the themes of the traditional Japanese garden; he draws on the mountains around and recreates their landscape. This goes beyond mere geometry; it is minimalistic perhaps but is filled with meaning and humour and a humane sympathy with the environment. A setting for scientific discourse has become a playground for adults, a place where scientific myth can hold sway.

163

Aerial view showing the car-park, with its "volcanoes" surmounted by junipers, and the approach to the Centre's buildings.

164

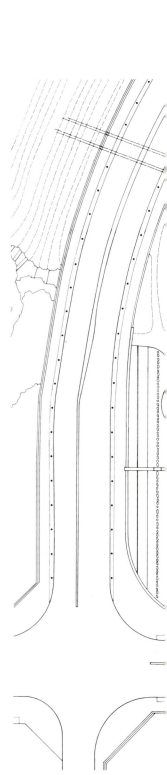

The moss mountain rises above the enclosing courtyard buildings and is set in a sea of gravel, offset by a square, gridded grove of bamboo; a line of stepping stones and stepped plank paths cross by.

In the plan the cones surmounted by junipers are at the top in the middle of the car-park; the stone and moss mountains are in the left-hand courtyard and the Director's garden is along the lower front of the building.

The Director's garden of lawn
and gravel with circular,
underlit pools and conifer
trees.

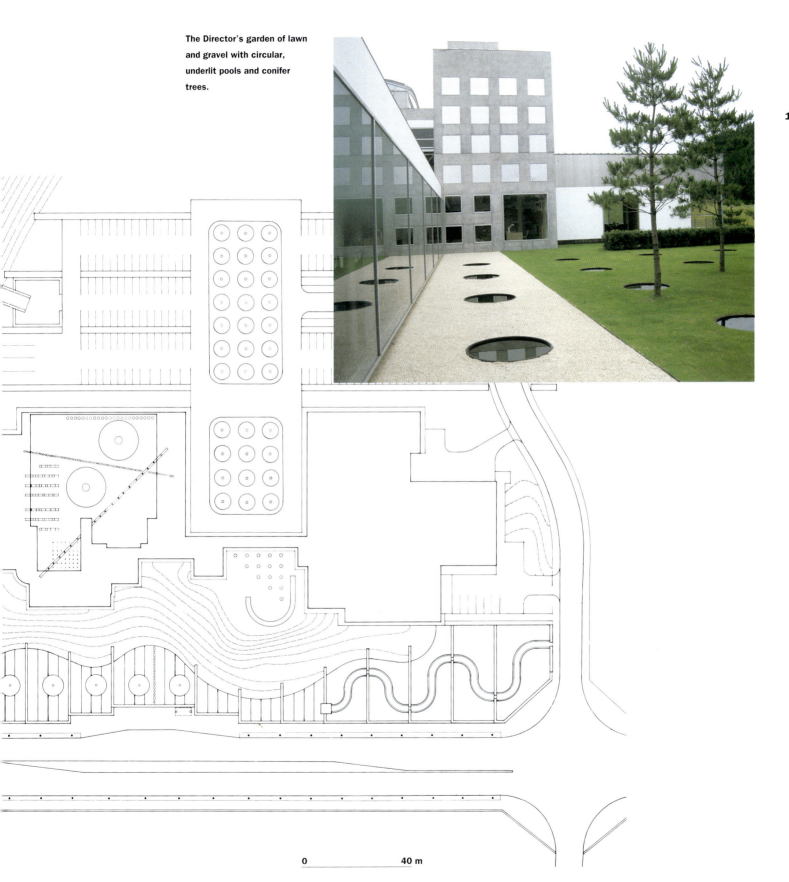

0   40 m

A straight, stepping-stone path
cuts across the area of grass,
lending tension to the design.

National Research Institute for Metals, Science and Technology

Tsukuba City, Ibaraki Prefecture, Japan

Shunmyo Masuno

Shunmyo Masuno has created a plaza from a space enclosed by buildings of the National Research Institute for Metals, Science and Technology. The plaza extends to promenades on the south side and on the south-east side a semicircular restaurant projects into the space.

The source of Masuno's design is man's quest for metal – as in the American Gold Rush men sought riches in dry, inhospitable mountain tops dotted with a few trees and dry river beds twisted across grassy plains. Prospectors would search for water and gather at springs. Like prospectors, the researchers at this institute tend to work alone, so the plaza is seen as a place where feelings of isolation and solitude may be relieved.

The area around the restaurant is paved in a square geometrical pattern of Chinese granite, interrupted by natural boulders of Korean granite and crossed by sinuous flows of gravel leading towards the restaurant. The boulders are granite from Hiroshima Prefecture and Aji stones from Kagawa Prefecture, and Masatoshi Izumi installed them under Shunmyo Masuno's direction. The formal pattern of the paving is gradually overtaken by undulating grass areas. A straight stepping-stone path cuts diagonally across the grassland and bridges the gravel riverbed in a curving single stone slab bridge. A spring, which is a low fountain, initiates the source of the dry river. This is landscape as metaphor and allegory, giving meaning to a place.

Shunmyo Masuno has created a plaza from a space enclosed by buildings of the National Metallurgical Research Institute. The plaza extends to promenades on the south side and on the south-east a semicircular restaurant projects into the space.

167

The rocks were chosen and positioned with care and understanding.

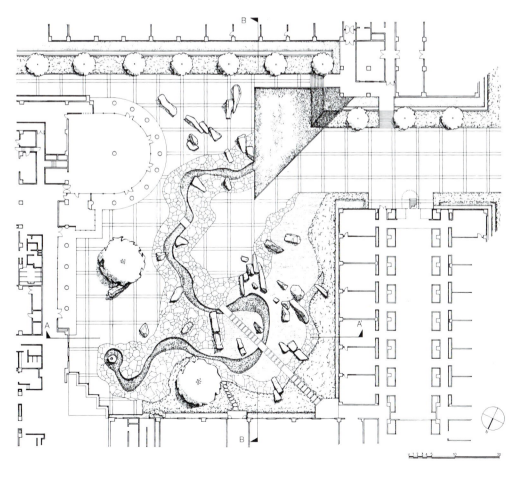

A mist fountain in the dry
river bed.

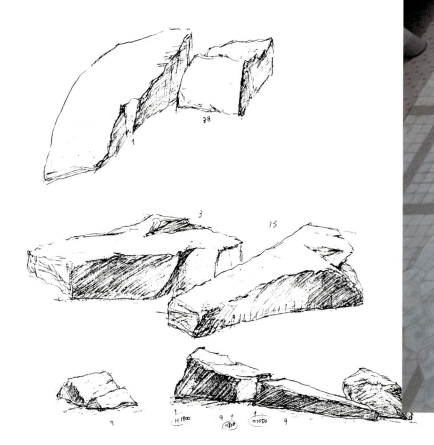

Shunmyo Masuno's
studies for the rock
positioning.

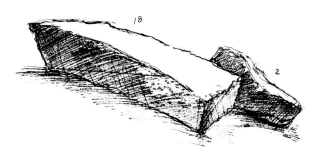

Looking south-east with the gridded, granite promenade to top left, crossed by the dry river which enters the green area, the whole plaza dotted by carefully positioned stones.

5.6
Forum Bonn

Bonn, Germany

Bödeker, Wagenfeld & Partner

This is a speculative office block built for the developer Moderne Stadt on Friedrich-Ebert Allee, the main north-south avenue running through Bonn which is lined with government buildings. It is a site close to the Rheinanenpark and just west of the 562 Rhine bridge, not far from the suburb of Bad Godesberg.

Friedrich-Ebert Allee lacks scale and composition and resembles a typical edge-of-town strip development, except that instead of crinkly-tin shopping parks and supermarkets it has much more up-market ministries, museums and office blocks. Part of the challenge of the design, therefore, was to establish a position and a sense of place. At Forum Bonn the answer has been to establish a solid, five-storey stone façade fronted by a matching stone pergola which will be clad in *Wisteria sinensis*. The pergola extends beyond the building across the whole frontage of the site and demarcates public and private space. It is approached by a semicircular drive, and two light glass structures project outwards from the main office building. One is an entrance way which penetrates the three-storey high square "window" punched through the façade. The other glass structure is a pyramid, surrounded by a moat and pointing to a water-lily pond nestling into *Robinia* trees at the back of the building.

Inside the building there is a high glazed atrium over an underground car-park. The paving of the atrium floor is lined by black stone bands that echo the structural grid of the building. Twelve semi-mature *Magnolia soulangeana* have been planted at intervals along the main building axis. These are underlit both by spotlights set into four linear planting beds and by underwater lights set into the central pool. This pool leads to a curved range of water steps which descend to the basement-level car-park.

Lighting is very important for this scheme. The pergola at the front is uplit by recessed sodium vapour discharge lights; the informally placed trees by the entrance drive are lit by coloured uplighters and the pyramid also shines out at night-time. This is a scheme which aims to create a presence, first by setting out a territory along an undistinguished urban highway, and secondly by creating within it usable social space, whether internal like the atrium or external like the pool next to the pyramid.

Opposite: The water steps which descend to the basement-level car-park.

The approach to the building, with semicircular drive and the stone-faced pergola which is planted with *Wisteria sinensis*.

The atrium pool with the rows of standard *Magnolia soulangeana* trees growing out of ground-cover beds of ivy.

The view out of the winter garden towards the rhododendron garden.

Research and Development Centre of the Heidelberger Druckmaschinen

Heidelberg, Germany

Georg Penker

Heidelberger Druckmaschinen makes printing machines and its new R. & D. centre is in central Heidelberg. The landscape design involves roof gardens at fourth-floor level which look out on to the Odenwald, and a first-floor winter garden which connects with external rose and rhododendron gardens. The internal winter garden has water channels set into the granite and porphyry paving, while internal galleries overlook the big *Ficus benjamina* trees.

Thus the building is furnished with a series of internal and external garden spaces. The winter garden is a meeting place and focus for the whole research centre and has a cafeteria. The two open garden courts beyond are quieter places for conversation and have pergolas which continue the rhythm of the structure of the building; in the rhododendron garden the pergolas are furnished with *Clematis*.

Each of the three gardens is square in plan and relates to a north-south axis through the three squares, which are also connected by water channels. The winter garden is organized to orientate on the two diagonals and the *Ficus* trees are slightly scattered. The rose garden is crossed by pergolas which divide it in four and the planting is comparatively informal; the rhododendron garden is totally informal and has serpentine paths. All the planting is raised and the structural constraints have required shallow pools and depths of soil.

The roof gardens serve the boardroom, but also repair the loss of biomass due to the development of the building. They include a pool and and some very attractive shrub, herbaceous and grass plant compositions and also allow views of the Odenwald. This belief that buildings should be literally green is common in Germany, but not taken sufficiently seriously worldwide.

The winter garden with its granite and porphyry paving, pool and *Ficus benjamina* trees. The space acts as a meeting place for the researchers.

Typha angustifolia emerges from the pool while *Miscanthus sinensis Gracillimus, Pennisetum compressum* and *Epilobium angustifolium* surround the water's edge and are backed by *Acer palmatum atropurpureum* and *Miscanthus sinensis giganterus*.

174

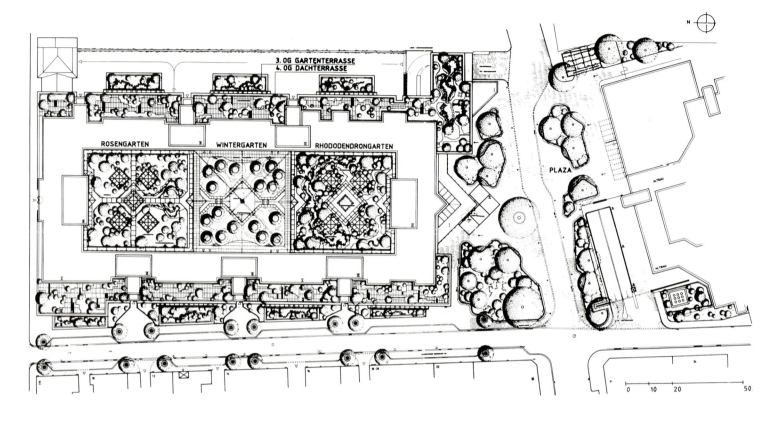

Site plan showing the
first-floor winter garden,
external rose and
rhododendron gardens and
rooftop garden.

The clematis-clad pergola in
the rhododendron garden.

The rooftop boardroom garden.

The entrance square with
limestone walls subdividing
the rippling lawn.

5.8

Shell Headquarters

Rueil, near Paris, France

Kathryn Gustafson

Aerial view of the model.

The Water Garden.

The entrance square and its waves of grass lawn.

The office buildings at the Shell Headquarters in Rueil enclose two sides of the entrance square. A path in limestone leads to the entrance of the complex at the junction of the two wings. To one side of the path lies a moat next to the building, and the water overflows towards the entrance path into a channel. The overflow is in green Brazilian granite. From the moat rise four stainless-steel masts which at the top become open spirals – at night flame-like lights make these masts appear like signals.

Most of the entrance square is occupied by undulating lawn which ripples in changing terraces down to the main entrance pathway. This lawn is subdivided by limestone walls which emerge and then disappear to re-emerge lower down. Six Japanese pagoda trees (*Sophora japonica*) also decorate the entrance courts.

Each of the two wings of the building has a number of lateral blocks which face away from the entrance square and contain linear courtyards enclosed on three sides. These courtyards are lined with parallel bands of lawn, shrubbery and ground cover creating soft, green, orchestrated gardens.

The moat continues under the main entrance and reappears as a cascade flowing into the Water Garden. Alongside the Water Garden is a linear bed of rhododendrons, camellias and azaleas. The planting palette follows the colours of the rainbow from white at the entrance (for example, *Magnolia stellata*) to blues and purple at the far end (for example, *Azalea Blue* Danube). On the other side of the glazed walkway from the Water Garden there is a series of pocket gardens. The colours of the Water Garden and the pocket gardens are co-ordinated so that white is with white (for example, *Rosa* "Iceberg", *Artemesia schmidtiana, Galium odoratum*), yellow is with yellow (*Robinia pseudoacacia Frisia, Hedera helix* "Buttercup", *Helianthemum nummularium*) and reds and oranges likewise (*Prunus pyracantha crenatoserrata* "Orange Glow", *Rosa* "Super Star" or *Polygonum offine* "Superbum").

Genentech Founders Research Center

San Francisco, California, USA

MPA Design, Michael Davies and David W. Nelson

This is a classic corporate "look-out" landscape built on top of a hill overlooking San Francisco Bay. Genentech's research centre consists of buildings designed by Jon Schlevning of SRG Partnership which are an exercise in crisp, gleaming white modernism. The three research buildings are set around a courtyard and there is an adjacent car-park structure.

Two of the buildings slide across each other to create an L-shaped space into which the third building juts at an acute angle. This creates the courtyard, which is actually a roof garden with a laboratory underneath. The juxtaposition of right-angled L-shape and one offset building generates lines and routes that radiate across the site. One main route becomes the 250-metre long, north-south axis, which descends across the site in a cascade of steps, terraces and ramps. To the east of the north-south axis is a gently curving route for wheelchairs, reached via a lift.

The planting design is informal and irregular. The bay-side landscape is open and dune-like to facilitate views of the water and the surrounding hills and Mount Diablo across the bay. The south and east sides are more heavily tree planted for wind shelter and to screen the adjacent street and parking lot views of the site.

Previously the site was unvegetated rocky banks and these have been completely reshaped. The courtyard was located at a height of 15 metres to provide bay views and yet allow access for the disabled from the higher-level parking lots. It is half a level below the visitor's arrival area and has a laboratory beneath it, so most of the courtyard is paved with removable 20 x 20 centimetre paviors

and with bands of slate. A semicircle of large, multi-stemmed trees in circular planters softens the paving. Below can be seen grass terraces and slopes and seashore planting of California natives, including grasses and succulent species in curvilinear patterns and land-shaped to recall a dune system. The steep slopes required careful maintenance to stop run-off and surface erosion until the plants were established, but after one year the slopes became secure.

This scheme is a classic of a landscape designer exploiting the potential of a site, articulating routes clearly and using plant species specific to a locality – in this case illustrating MPA's command of the use of drought-tolerant plants.

The mid-point of the "dune meadow" with the north-south stairway and courtyard beyond. San Francisco Bay is on the left.

Opposite: "Dune meadow" viewed from the area east of the main courtyard. Dune grass is on 50 per cent slopes, the curving areas of lawns are on gentle slopes and the lower three areas are informally linked.

View from Point San Bruno Boulevard, Building 17 and the courtyard of the Founders Research Center.

180

Views from the north-east terrace overlooking a semi-circular terrace with multi-stemmed Japanese maple trees. The colour of Mount San Bruno and dune grass are similar and help to connect the site in the summer to hills of dry grass.

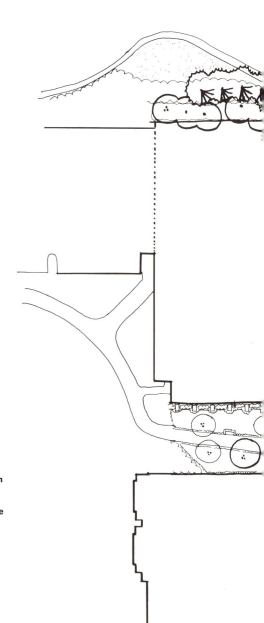

Seats under the Japanese maples.

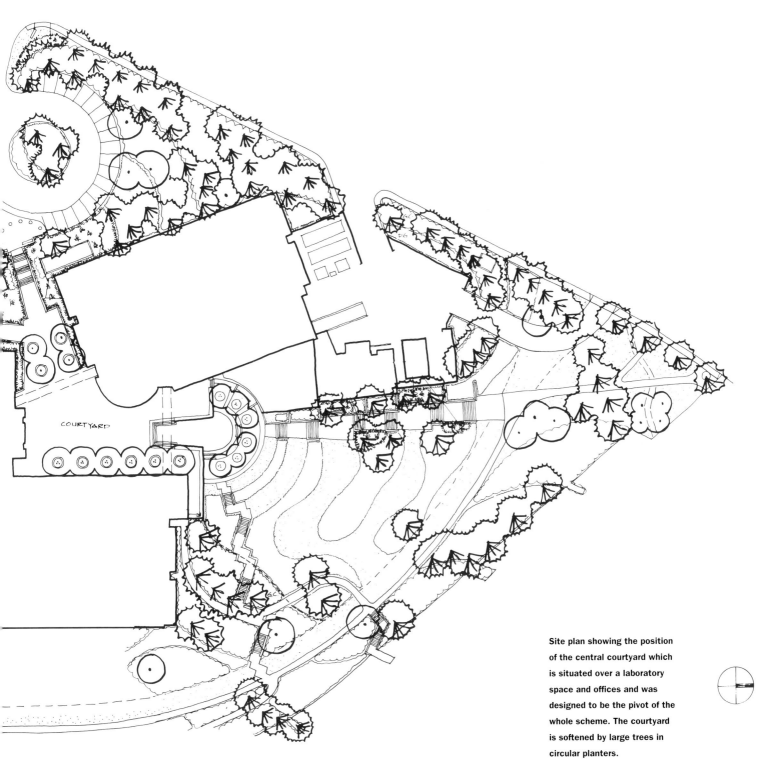

COURTYARD

Site plan showing the position
of the central courtyard which
is situated over a laboratory
space and offices and was
designed to be the pivot of the
whole scheme. The courtyard
is softened by large trees in
circular planters.

5.10
Process Science Center

San Francisco, California, USA

MPA Design, Michael Painter

This project was a continuation of MPA's design work for Genentech, following its involvement in the Founders Research Center from 1990 to 1992 (see page 179). The Process Science Center is also in South San Francisco overlooking the Bay and consists of a long, thin courtyard 25 x 166 metres, divided into two by a bridge between buildings at first-storey level. One side of the bridge is hard paved; the other side is mainly soft and planted. The scheme aims to enhance views of the Bay and block out undesirable aspects.

Genentech has scientists and engineers who are very interested in design and voice their views, likes and dislikes strongly. So the landscape designers worked closely with employees through an approvals process at various levels of the company from building facility engineering, building plant maintenance, security and user groups to vice president and president. After the project was completed there was a project review of the success, failures and shortcomings.

The source of the design is the double helix, the DNA molecule, expanded 40 billion times to create a triple ellipse shape large enough to be seen from the air after take-off from San Francisco Airport. Genentech uses the double helix in its PR information.

The courtyard was formed when a new building (by Bill Bula of Flad and Associates) was sited next to an existing building. The designers sited the new building off-parallel so the space widens out slightly towards the Bay while the helix shapes conversely narrow. Furthermore, the ground level of the courtyard is tilted down from the bridge to the Bay end.

The helix is represented by two paths. The broader path that slopes uniformly towards the bay is in lightly sand-blasted concrete. The narrow path undulates in level and is heavily sand-blasted to reveal the texture and colour of the limestone aggregate which matches the colour of the precast cladding of the building. The grass ellipses are bermed, and green slate paviors are set in lines angled at 45 degrees which connect the helix. The entry courtyard is completely paved with 200 x 200 centimetre Hanover paviors forming the background to the helix pattern and bands of green slate alternating with narrow, black slate bands, again set at 45 degrees. The courtyard has coastal plants including dune grass, cypress, pine and oak trees, blue-flowering ceanothus, orange poppies and purple sea lavender.

The progressive reduction in the size of the three segments of double helix creates a false perspective and makes the courtyard seem longer. The undulation of earth forms, curving walks and plants creates a feeling of both shelter and motion as the occasional breeze moves the grasses.

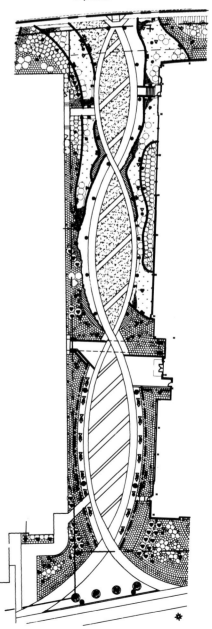

Plan. The bottom ellipse is paved.

Opposite: Rooftop view of the helix courtyard.

Above: Paving and grass intertwine in patterns full of meaning.

Opposite: Ground-level view of the helix courtyard.

The paved helix courtyard by the main building lobby with a bridge connection to Building 5. 200 x 200-centimetre paviors with wide bands of green slate alternate with narrow bands of black slate.

Biographies & Company Profiles

Aspinwall Clouston, BCP Far East Sendirian Berhad, No. 32.1 Jalan Sambanthan 3, Brickfields, 50470 Kuala Lumpur, Malaysia
Aspinwall Clouston was formed in 1992 when Aspinwall and Clouston merged with Clouston Asia. Today, with offices in the UK, Hong Kong, Singapore and Kuala Lumpur, the practice is one of the world's leading environmental management consultancies offering services in planning, urban design and landscape architecture. Work currently being undertaken includes projects in Vietnam, Indonesia, The Maldives, China and Macau. Aspinwall Clouston has been internationally recognized, receiving design awards for landscape and planning schemes such as the Jordan Valley Urban Fringe Park Feasibility Study, Hong Kong, which was given the Award of Merit for Planning from the Institute of Landscape Architects (1991) and the UK Landscape Institute Prize (1993). The firm is also active in environmental impact assessments for proposed new developments, including waste-disposal facilities (an area of expertise since the formation of Aspinwall's Asian operation in 1988), power stations, roads, railways, manufacturing plants and recreational schemes. Recent projects include the Sha Tin Town Park and the Waterfront Park at Butterfly Beach. The firm also created the simulated tropical valleys of Jurong Bird Park, Singapore, and has completed landscape designs for civic spaces, institutions, residential areas, industrial sites, commercial buildings, transport routes, hotels and resorts.

Batlle i Roig, Arquitectes, Provença 355, 5è 1a, 08037 Barcelona, Spain Batlle i Roig was founded in 1981 by Enric Batlle i Durany and Joan Roig i Duran. Both graduated from ETSAB (Barcelona School of Architecture) and served apprenticeships under Torres Lapeña. Their landscape design work has won considerable acclaim within Spain and they have three times been awarded the Premios FAD de Arquitectura: in 1985 for the Roques Blanques Metropolitan Cemetery, in 1994 for the Trinitat Park, Barcelona, and in 1995 for the Malniu area redevelopment scheme in Girona.

Bödeker, Wagenfeld & Partner, Bergische Landstrasse 606, 40629 Düsseldorf, Germany
Formed in 1971 by Richard Bödeker, Armin Boyer (left in 1995) and Horst Wagenfeld, BW&P is a group of landscape architects and planners specializing in all fields relating to landscape design. Where necessary they work alongside other experts in fields such as environmental protection, forestry, land and water management, nature and landscape conservation and with town planners, architects and civil engineers. Their work can be seen throughout Europe, the Middle East and the Gulf States, and the company employs a resident team in Saudi Arabia to co-ordinate and supervise ongoing landscape construction sites. BW&P is a member of various landscape institutions within Germany, including the International Federation of Landscape Architects, and the Federation of German Landscape Architects, and it has received national awards for its research work. Many of BW&P's commissions arise from national competitions, such as the urban open space planning Agrarian Community Competition; the planning for the Ministry of Foreign Affairs, staff housing, Saudi Arabia; the Botanical Garden in Bochum, Germany; the VEBA Oil Administration Centre; the German Embassy, Teheran, and numerous private residences in Germany, elsewhere in Europe and the Middle East.

Bureau B + B, Herengracht 252, 1016 BV, Amsterdam, The Netherlands Bureau B + B was founded in 1977 by Riek Bakker and Ank Bleeker who have since left to start practices elsewhere. Today the Amsterdam-based firm employs 20 staff and concentrates mainly on urban planning. Early projects include the Concours International du Parc de la Villette; the planning of the Noorder-ij-Polder Lake near Amsterdam; tourist recreational structural plans for Rotterdam, and the Archeon theme park in Alphen-on-the-Rhine. Since the mid-1980s Bureau B + B has become increasingly involved in consulting activities, liaising closely with local authorities in the redesign of public areas, for example, "The Healthy Core" redeployment of the inner city of The Hague. Other areas of expertise include parks, cemeteries, forecourts and rural land reclamation.

Robert Camlin, Camlin Lonsdale, Parc Bach, Llangadfan, Powys SY21 0PL, Wales, UK Robert Camlin received his landscape training as a local government officer in Northern Ireland between 1972 and 1979. He studied at Manchester Polytechnic, then worked as a freelance designer in France and the UK and as a landscape consultant with a Manchester-based studio. In 1989 he started a partnership with Tom

Lonsdale. In addition to his private practice he has served as Landscape Institute Representative on Manchester City Council Historic Buildings and Conservation Areas Panel and has acted as visiting tutor and critic at Cambridge, Edinburgh Herriot-Watt, Oxford Brooks, Manchester Metropolitan and Liverpool Universities.

Child Associates Inc., Landscape Architects, 240 Newbury Street, Boston, Massachusetts 02116, USA Child Associates was created by Susan Child who trained at Radcliffe Institute, Cambridge, Massachusetts, receiving a Master of Arts Certificate in Landscape and Environmental Design (1975), and the Harvard University Graduate School of Design, receiving a Master of Landscape Architecture (1981). To date the practice has designed a number of significant urban projects, including the award-winning waterfront parks at Battery Park City, New York – South Cove Park (1989) in collaboration with Mary Miss, artist, and Stan Eckstut, architect; and North Cove Link Park (1995) with Mitchell/ Giurgola Architects and Martin Puryear, sculptor, which received an American Institute of Architects National Award for urban design. The firm is also involved in the landscaping of campus sites (New Clinical Center of Beth Israel Hospital, Boston, due for completion in 1996); historic preservation (masterplan for the Stan Hywet Hall Foundation, Akron, Ohio, which received both the American Society of Landscape Architects and the Boston Society of Landscape Architects honour awards), and private residential garden design throughout the north-east and the mid-west of the United States. Susan Child currently serves on the Boston Civic Design Commission. She has participated in two national and three regional faculties for the Mayors' Institute on City Design sponsored by the National Endowment for the Arts. She has served on numerous design juries and symposiums, has been a guest teacher and critic at the Harvard University Graduate School of Design and has lectured widely on various topics in landscape architecture.

Arkitektgruppen Cubus, Rosenkrantzgaten 3, Bergen N-5003, Norway Cubus, a practice employing architects, landscape architects, planners, social scientists and civil engineers, was founded more than 20 years ago. It is involved in consumer participation, co-operative forms of housing, building design and planning, construction management and urban and landscape planning. During the last ten years Cubus has received a number of architectural awards, and has also won several local and national competitions. These include the

European Construction Prize for homes built for the Seamen's Housing Association, Bergen (1982); the Houen's Fund Prize (Norway's most prestigious architectural award) for Loddefjord School, Bergen (1988), and the Det Nyttige Selskap's prize for excellent architecture for the Allers Building (1990).

DENruijter.etc., Postbus 297, 6950 AG Dieren, The Netherlands Michiel den Ruijter combines the disciplines of landscape architecture, urban design and the arts, and his work is always strongly influenced by the existing landscape. His practice specializes in rural and urban public spaces and has worked on world exhibitions, new towns, land reclamation, new woods, waterfronts, nature parks and outdoor arts projects. All the principals of the company are involved in education, one being the chairman of the European Master of Landscape Architecture (EMLA) course, a co-operation between several European universities.

Eachus Huckson, 7 Church Street, Kidderminster, Worcestershire DY10 2AD, UK Eachus Huckson was founded in 1981 and offers services in landscape design and planning. The consultancy has major clients in both the private and public sectors throughout the UK, Europe and the Middle East, including British Telecom; Birmingham City Council; the Countryside Commission; Garden Festival Wales; the National Trust; McDonald's, and Esso Petroleum Company Plc. The practice has achieved national acclaim, receiving awards from the Civic Trust and the Association for Landscape Industries, and has expertise in both large-scale landscape planning and the detailed design of hard and soft landscapes. Recent schemes include the Palace Garden, Jeddah; the Law Courts, Wolverhampton; Lake and Lakeside Area, Garden Festival Wales, and the British Garden at the Floriade, The Netherlands (1992).

EcoSystems, PO Box 737, Nightcliff NT 0810, Australia EcoSystems offers site planning, landscape and urban design, and environmental planning and management services to a wide range of clients from Commonwealth and Territory Government to local and international bodies. The practice often collaborates with Landplan Studio, a Brisbane-based firm of landscape architects with international experience in the UK, Japan and south-east Asia. EcoSystems' projects include the Seven Spirit Wilderness, Arnhem Land, Northern Territory, which won the Australian Government Tourism Award and the Award in Landscape Excellence from the Australian Institute of Landscape Architects; the Katherine Power Station; Stage 1 landscape to the New Parliament House, Darwin, Fannie Bay Precinct; the Alice Springs townscape plan, and the Stuart Highway from Arnhem Highway to Berrimah.

Principal of EcoSystems, David Metcalfe, was educated at the University of New South Wales, later completing qualifying examinations for the Australian Institute of Landscape Architects.

EDAW Inc., 753 Davis Street, San Francisco, California 94111, USA EDAW has been a leading name in international landscape planning and urban design for the last 50 years and has offices throughout the USA and Australia as well as in the UK, France and Hong Kong. Most of the practice's work involves large-scale design projects, and clients range from corporations and institutions to public agencies and architectural firms. EDAW has received over 120 awards from local, state and national professional organizations in the last 20 years.

Environment Design Institute, Mita Sonnette Bldg 3F, 1-1-15 Mita, Minato-ku, Tokyo 108, Japan Mitsuru Man Senda (b. 1941 in Yokohama) was the Head of the Environment Design Institute from 1968 to 1984 during which time he gained a doctorate in engineering. He graduated from the Architectural Department of the Tokyo Institute of Technology in 1964, then spent four years in the practice of Kiyonori Kikutake Architects and Associates. He has held various teaching positions in Japan and today is Professor of Architecture in the Engineering Department of the Tokyo Institute. He has received various prizes within Japan and in 1993 was awarded the Architectural Institute of Japan Kazumigaseki Memorial Prize and Grand Expo Prize, Supreme Order of Merit, for his Shinshu Expo Alpiko Plaza.

Environmental Design Partnership, PO Box 2425, Randburg 2125, South Africa Environmental Design Partnership was formed in south Africa in 1981 when Gareth and Sarah Singleton moved there to represent a British firm of landscape architects. EDP now has four directors, all of whom are British, employing over 25 staff, making it one of the largest environmental service teams in Southern Africa. Projects have been undertaken throughout the African States from offices based in Johannesburg, Durban, Botswana, Namibia and Swaziland. The workload is extremely varied with the main disciplines of operation being resource and environmental planning, tourism and recreation planning, landscape architecture and urban design. Over 600 commissions have been undertaken, including an environmental impact assessment for the expansion of Mbabane and Manzini in Swaziland, and the creation of a game reserve on a 120-hectare corporate headquarters.

Eric Fulford, 685 Middle Drive, Woodruff Place, Indianapolis, Indiana 46201, USA Eric Fulford is a landscape architect with experience in designing public spaces. His work is inspired by his love for industrial ruins and materials which can be seen in projects such as his unbuilt masterplan for the White River State Park. With his wife, Ann Fulford Reed, he is a partner in the firm ROAMworks in Indianapolis, Indiana, which specializes in domestic garden design. Fulford received a Bachelor of Science degree from Oregon State University, a Master of Landscape Architecture from the University of Illinois and a Dip.UDRP from the University of Edinburgh, Scotland. He is a Fellow of the American Academy in Rome.

Grupo de Diseño Urbano, Fernando Montes de Oca 4, Colonia Condesa, 06140 Mexico City, Mexico D.F. The Mexico City-based Grupo de Diseño Urbano was founded in 1977 by Mario Schjetnan and José Luis Pérez, since which time the practice has become internationally recognized for its creative and innovative work in landscape architecture, architecture and urban design in both the public and private sectors. The emphasis of GDU's work is on large-scale public projects collaborating with specialists in art, social sciences, economics, finance, ecology and civil and systems engineering. The practice works entirely in Mexico, and recent landscape projects include the Parque Tezozomoc, Xochimilco; the Culhuacan Historical Archaeological Park; and the Ciudad Solidaridad Urban Centre. Environmental planning and masterplans number the Bahias de Huatulco Tourist Development, Oaxaca; the Cerro Prieto Industrial and Geothermal Park, Baja, California, and the masterplan for the National Medical Centre, Mexico City. Also active in architecture and housing, GDU has recently completed Quinta Eugenia Housing Project, Mexico City; the Museum of Modern Art, Toluca, and the Museo de las Culturas del Norte, Paquimé, Casas Grandes, Coahuila, amongst others. GDU has received various national awards, including an Honour Award for the Parque Ecologico Xochimilco from the Mexican Federation of Architects, as well as citations on three occasions from the American Society of Landscape Architects, most recently in 1994 for the Parque Xochimilco.

Kathryn Gustafson, 9 rue Elisabeth, 94200 Ivry sur Seine, France Kathryn Gustafson studied at the University of Washington, the Fashion Institute of Technology, New York and the Ecole Nationale Supérieure du Paysage, Versailles. She worked in fashion design for seven years but since 1980 has been employed as a freelance landscape architect. In 1993 she received a Médaille d'Architecture from the Académie d'Architecture for her work. Gustafson is well known in France but has also worked in The Netherlands and the USA and her designs have been exhibited nationally, most recently at the Musée d'Art Moderne in Paris. Projects include Vias seaside park (1991); an urban boulevard at Gennevilliers (1991); the Evangile park, Paris (1991); the exterior spaces of the L'Oréal factory, Aulnay la Barbière (1992); the landscaping of the headquarters of Shell at Rueil-Malmaison and also of Esso; the Terrasson Park (1995), and the Contemporary Art Museum at Tours (1995). She has also completed several designs and study plans, including the EDF electrical pylons and the Barrage at Nancy. Currently Gustafson is working with the architects HOK on the San Francisco International Airport, and with Norman Foster on the Grand Stade, Saint-Denis.

Hammel Green and Abrahamson Landscape Architecture Group, 1201 Harmon Place, Minneapolis, Minnesota 55403-1985, USA

The HGA Landscape Architecture Group was established in 1986 to provide site planning and landscape architectural design within the parent firm of Hammel Green and Abrahamson Inc. Since this time the practice has gained a national reputation on a variety of projects from small gardens to corporate and university campuses. In 1995 it received a Merit Award in Planning from the American Society of Landscape Architects for the design of the Memorial Park Arboretum and Gardens in Appleton, Wisconsin.

Hargreaves Associates, 539 Bryant Street, Third Floor, San Francisco, California 94123, USA

George Hargreaves was educated at the University of Georgia School of Environmental Design and at the Harvard University Graduate School of Design, receiving a Bachelor of Landscape Architecture, Magna Cum Laude (1976) and a Master of Landscape with Distinction (1979). He worked initially for the Cheshire Design Group in England before joining the SWA Group in Sausalito, California and forming his own company, Hargreaves Associates. The practice is a consulting firm comprised of landscape architects and planners offering a wide range of services, including urban design, planning, commercial and office projects, industrial and research facility design, park and recreational planning and design, and public commissions. Current work includes several public parks such as phases of the Guadalupe River Park in San Jose, California; the Louisville Waterfront Park, Kentucky, and the Columbus Center, Baltimore, Maryland. George Hargreaves is an Adjunct Professor at the Harvard University Graduate School of Design and is visiting professor/critic at many institutions across the USA. He has sat on international

panels and in 1988 was the chairman of the American Society of Landscape Architects' Professional Awards of Excellence. He has published and exhibited his own works widely.

Heads Co. Ltd, Osaka, Japan Heads was founded in 1967 as Ohtsuka Landscape Gardening Design Office Ltd, changing to its present name in 1969. Today it employs over 50 personnel and has offices in Osaka, Tokyo and New York. The company's activities cover a broad spectrum, including surveying, designing and supervising the landscaping of institutional, recreational and industrial complexes. It is also involved in the survey, research and design of large-scale projects such as land development and comprehensive urban planning. Heads Co. is a member of the Japan Landscape Consultants Association, the Parks and Open Spaces Association of Japan and the Japanese Institute of Landscape Architects. Recent design prizes include the Best Award in the Seventh Urban Park Competition from the Ministry of Construction for the Kouhoku, Yamazaki District Park (1991) and a Japanese Landscape Consultant Committee award for the Akibadai Park scheme (1993).

Internationale Bauausstellung Emscher Park, GmbH, Leitherstrasse 35, 45886 Gelsenkirchen, Germany The IBA was founded in 1989 to coordinate the landscaping of the Emscher district, which upon completion will encompass over 92 projects in five central working fields in the northern Ruhr district of Germany. It operates as a wholly owned subsidiary of the Land North Rhine-Westphalia but has limited liability. A total of 30 people are employed at the IBA, including general management, operations and public relations departments. The work of the IBA is supported by a board of directors consisting of professors from various disciplines. Decisions relating to the admission of projects are taken by the Ministry of Urban Development and Transport of North Rhine-Westphalia and the steering committee is composed of members of the land departments, the member towns, industry and the trade unions and from nature conservation, planning and architects' associations.

Ronald Izumita, IMA Design Group Inc., 17992 Mitchell South, Irvine, California 92714, USA Ronald Izumita trained at the California State Polytechnic University and at the Harvard University Graduate School of Design, receiving Bachelor of Science and Master's degrees in Landscape Architecture. He has been involved in landscape architecture for over 30 years, during which time he has been honoured with a Fellowship of the American Society of Landscape Architects in 1990, and the Most Distinguished

Alumni of the Year Award from California State Polytechnic University, Pomona (1988). He joined IMA Design Group as its president and co-founder after serving as a Senior Principal with Peridian from 1991 to 1993.

Kinnear Landscape Architects, 113-117 Farringdon Road, London EC1R 3BT, UK. Lynn Kinnear worked in various landscape practices before studying landscape architecture at Edinburgh College of Art/Heriot-Watt, receiving a Bachelor of Arts degree in 1983. She was made an Associate of the Landscape Institute in 1985 and established her own firm in 1991. She has been a senior lecturer at Greenwich University since 1993. Completed work includes projects in the London Docklands, whilst recent planned schemes number the Scottish Equitable Headquarters and a landscape policy reassessment for J. Sainsbury Plc. In 1994 Lynn Kinnear was awarded first place in the Bangour Hospital Redevelopment competition, Scotland.

Landscape Design Associates, 17 Minster Precincts, Peterborough PE1 1XX, UK The landscape architecture, urban design and environmental planning company Landscape Design Associates is based in Peterborough with a project office in Leeds. The range of work undertaken by the practice varies from regional landscape planning, landscape assessments and environmental impact assessments to the detailed design, implementation and management of individual landscape schemes. Specialist areas include new settlements, masterplanning, offices and business parks, housing, roads, urban renewal, countryside management, habitat creation and forest planning. The practice is well known for its innovative ideas and the directors are familiar figures on the international conference circuit. Clients come from both the public and private sectors and include government departments, local authorities, the Countryside Commission, English Nature, housing associations and major British landowners.

Landscape Group, Hong Kong Housing Authority, Hong Kong The Landscape Group was founded in 1977 and remained a one-man operation until 1981 when it expanded. Today the department employs three senior landscape architects as well as eleven designers, one assistant and a support team of sixteen. Their current workload covers more than 300 projects, about 30 per cent of which are delegated to approved consultant landscape firms. The majority of work is involved with the design, construction and planting of external areas of public housing estates, although the department occasionally designs public parks.

Latitude Nord, 44-46 rue de Domrémy, 75013 Paris, France Laurence Vacherot and Gilles Vexlard, joint directors of the Paris-based Latitude Nord, both trained at the Ecole Nationale Supérieure d'Horticulture de Versailles. They work primarily on urban projects, sometimes in an advisory capacity, but are often involved directly in long-term schemes which include town planning, leisure and sports facilities and the development of historic sites. This diversity has led them to employ a team of specialists in areas such as ecology, lighting effects and agronomy. Projects include the redevelopment of the Place de la Comédie, Montpellier, and the medieval village of Valbonne; the Place Charles de Gaulle, Paris; the Miramas and Voisins-Bretonnex districts, as well as leisure centres at Verneuil, Bois-le-Roi, Mousseaux and Draveil. Gilles Vexlard is a consultant for the Direction Départementale de l'Equipement du Nord and professor at the Ecole Nationale Supérieure du Paysage.

Latz + Partner, Landschaftsarchitekten, Ampertshausen 6, D-85402 Kranzberg, Germany Latz + Partner was founded in 1968 and established offices in Aachen and Saarbrücken. The firm moved in 1973 following Peter Latz's appointment as lecturer at the University of Kassel, and in 1984 opened a further office in Freising when Latz joined the staff of the University of Munich. The Duisburg office opened in 1991. As well as the directors Peter Latz and Anneliese Latz, the practice has nine collaborating landscape architects in Kranzberg and Duisburg. The firm is involved mainly in landscape architecture, planning and urban design and its work has been published nationally.

Legorreta Arquitectos, Palacio de Versalles 285 A, 11020 Mexico D.F. Ricardo Legorreta was educated at the Universidad Nacional Autónoma de México. He is well known for his use of light and shade, water and texture, hard edges and fluid lines and is as much involved with the creation of private living spaces as with the design of major buildings for hotels, offices and factories. Early work was completed entirely in Mexico but he is now recognized internationally as a leading architect. Important projects include the Solana business campus and resort, Dallas; Camino Real hotels in Mexico City; the Museum of Modern Art in Monterrey, Mexico; the Managua Cathedral, Nicaragua; the International Student Center at the University of California, Los Angeles, and the Children's Museum in Mexico City. Schemes currently in progress include Televisa, Mexico; the Tech Museum of Innovation, San Jose, California, and the masterplan and First Phase design of Chiron Corporation's Life

Sciences Programme, Emeryville, California. Legorreta was recently honoured with the International Award for the Architect of the Americas and he is an Honorary Fellow of the American Institute of Architects.

John Lyle, 580 N. Hermosa, Sierra Madre, California 91024, USA John Lyle is Professor of Landscape Architecture at the California State Polytechnic University in Pomona. He teaches and practises ecological planning and design and was the founder of the Center for Regenerative Studies, guiding its development until 1994. His 606 Studio has carried out planning projects for local, state, federal and international agencies exploring the potential of regenerative processes for achieving sustainability. He has received or shared nine national awards from the American Society of Landscape Architects and has published his ideas widely. Lyle is a Fellow of the American Society of Landscape Architects, was named Outstanding Educator by the Council of Educators in Landscape Architecture in 1989 and has received the Honor Award for professional achievement from the California Council of Landscape Architects.

Shunmyo Masuno, Japan Landscape Consultants Co. Ltd, Kenkohji 1-2-1 Baba, Tsurumi-ku, Yokohama City 230, Japan Shunmyo Toshiaki Masuno studied at the Agricultural Faculty of Tamagawa University in Tokyo. After graduating in 1975 he became a pupil at Katsuo Saito, for whom he had worked while studying. In 1979 Masuno entered Daihonzansojiji Temple where he underwent ascetic training to become a priest. He established Japan Landscape Consultants in 1982 and became assistant resident priest at Kenkoji Temple in 1985. In 1987 he was invited by the University of British Columbia, Vancouver to give a series of lectures as a visiting professor. He also lectured at Cornell and Toronto Universities in 1989 and at the Harvard University Graduate School of Design in 1990. Masuno was presented with an Award of Merit by the University of British Columbia for his design and implementation of the restoration of the Nitobe Memorial Garden early in 1994 and was appointed an adjunct professor at the same university. Recent domestic projects include the National Research Institute for Metals, Science and Technology, Ibaraki Prefecture; Niigata Prefectural Museum of Modern Art; the first federally owned senior citizens' home, Chiba Prefecture; the redevelopment of Nakano 4-chome east area, as well as the Headquarters of Marui Co. and residential building, Nakano, Tokyo. Completed work abroad includes Phase 1 for the Canadian Museum of Civilization, Ottawa, and the Peace Park at Wewak in Papua New Guinea.

MBM Arquitectes SA, Placa Reial 18, Pral., 08002 Barcelona, Spain MBM Arquitectes was founded by Josep Martorell and Oriol Bohigas in 1951. David Mackay joined the partnership in 1962, and Albert Puigdomenech in 1986. With a staff of around 25 the firm has handled over 300 architecture and urban planning and design schemes during the last 40 years, working in Mexico, France, Germany, The Netherlands, Italy, Scotland and Wales. Recent projects include the Olympic Village and Olympic Port in Barcelona and the main pavilion for Expo'92 Seville. The practice has taken part in numerous international competitions, frequently being awarded first prize. Current projects include housing in Breda, The Netherlands (1995); Bite Avenue and Square in Cardiff (1994); urban design studies for Edinburgh waterfront (1995), and urban planning studies with new photovoltaic/thermal building components for the Directorate General, Science, Research and Development – European Commission (1995). Josep Martorell and Oriol Bohigas studied together before founding MBM. Martorell was the head of the architectural department of the Vila Olimpica, guiding the urban design of the scheme. Bohigas was head of the Barcelona School of Architecture from 1977 to 1980 at which time he became chief architect and planner of the first democratic government of the city.

MPA, 414 Mason Street, San Francisco, California, USA MPA Design is a landscape and urban design practice based in San Francisco. It was established in 1969 as Michael Painter and Associates and since then has successfully completed over 600 masterplanning and landscape design projects throughout the United States and abroad. Projects vary from courtyards, parks and plazas to masterplans for large sites with phased development for streetscapes, campuses, corporate facilities, new communities and resort areas. Michael Painter was educated at the University of California at Berkeley and the Harvard Graduate School of Design, where he obtained a Master of Landscape Design degree in urban design in 1966. Since founding MPA he has been awarded many regional and national design awards and is a frequent lecturer and panellist at Harvard University and the College of Environmental Design, Berkeley. He is a former Chairman of the American Society of Landscape Architects. Major schemes undertaken by MPA include the Great Highway Ocean Beach, California; Pacific Bell San Ramon Administration Center; Spanish Bay at Pebble Beach; the Genentech's Founders Research Center and Process Science Laboratory, San Francisco; UC Berkeley's Foothill Undergraduate Housing; and Dan Foley Community Park in Vellejo.

Nikken Sekkei Ltd, 1-4-27 Koraku, Bunkyo-ku, Tokyo 112, Japan Nikken Sekkei Ltd is Japan's largest architectural engineering consulting firm, providing services in project planning, design and construction administration for architecture, engineering and city planning. Since its formation in 1900 it has grown steadily to become a major, multi-discipline design organization with nearly 1,800 permanent professionals and support staff. Nikken has handled more than 13,000 projects to date, including overseas operations since 1964, and has expanded its field of activity to 40 countries. Nikken has received many national and international awards for design, engineering and planning. Recent planning schemes include Tsukuba Science Park (1994); Kansai Science City (1994), and Tanabe Campus, Doshisha University, Kyoto (1994).

Lea Nørgaard & Vibeke Holscher Landscape Architects, Godthabsvej 7, DK 2000 Frederiksberg C, Denmark The architectural firm Edith and Ole Nørgaard was established in 1954. Today the company is led by Lea Nørgaard, architect (b. 1952) and Vibeke Holscher, landscape architect (b. 1948), under the name of Lea Nørgaard & Vibeke Holscher Landscape Architects. Their work involves mainly large-scale public commissions; education and research institutions; administration, industrial and cultural buildings; planning and urban renewal. Major schemes include work for IBM in Brussels and Lundote; the Louisiana Museum of Modern Art, Humlebæk, and the planning and redevelopment of an old gravel-mining site into the "Hedeeland" regional park and recreation area south-west of Copenhagen. Nørgaard obtained a Master's degree in architecture in 1978 and is a member of both the Danish Architects Association and the Society of Danish Landscape Architects; Holscher has a Master's degree in architecture (1973) and is a member of the Society of Danish Landscape Architects.

Olin Partnership, 421 Chestnut Street, Philadelphia, Pennsylvania 19106, USA Hanna/Olin (now known as the Olin Partnership) was created in 1976, since which time it has established an international reputation as an innovative landscape architecture practice. Clients range from renowned architects to planners, public agencies, corporations, institutions, development groups and foundations worldwide. The practice is active in environmental analysis, master and site planning and landscape design, working on mixed use urban developments, corporate headquarters, educational and cultural institutions, public parks and civic spaces. Hanna/Olin's principals, Laurie Olin and Dennis McGlade, have had their designs published in

many professional journals and magazines and have received major awards in landscape architecture, including national design awards from the American Society of Landscape Architects and the American Institute of Architects and *Progressive Architecture* magazine, as well as the Bard award for Civic Design Excellence from the City Club of New York City. Both partners are involved in teaching landscape architecture, planning and design and are well-known figures on the international lecturing circuit.

Georg Penker, Hermann-Klammt-Strasse 3, 41460 Neuss, Germany Georg Penker studied at the Technische Universität München, opening his own office in Neuss, Düsseldorf in 1958 and a branch office in Brandenburg in 1994. Currently the practice employs 16 full-time designers. The majority of Penker's work is in the areas of landscape design and environmental planning and his aim is to harmonize nature and civilization. Completed projects include the University of Düsseldorf; the North Rhine-Westphalia Parliament in Düsseldorf and the Rhein Promenade in Cologne. He has received many national awards for his work and is a member of both the Bund Deutscher Landschaftsarchitekten (BDLA) and the Deutsche Gesellschaft für Gartenkunst und Landschaftspflege (DGGL).

Rundell Ernstberger Associates, 315 South Jefferson Street, Muncie, Indiana 47305, USA Rundell Ernstberger Associates was established in 1979 and provides land-planning, urban design and landscape architectural services specializing in masterplanning and site design. Work includes campus planning at various universities throughout the United States; corporate facilities site design such as Eli Lilly in Indianapolis; recreation planning for Standing Stone State Rustic Park in Tennessee, Lake Barkley in Tennessee and Kentucky, and the Monon Rail/Trail in Indianapolis; riverfront developments, and urban design in Albuquerque, New Mexico, and Colchester, Vermont. The practice has also undertaken masterplans for the relocated Highway 218 Corridor, Iowa; the Wabash River through five Indiana counties; and speciality planning and design for the Ball Brothers Foundation Minnetrista Cultural Center and the Commons at the New Indianapolis Zoo.

Alain Sarfati – AREA, 28 rue Barbet de Jouy, 75007 Paris, France Architect and town planner Alain Sarfati was born in 1937. In 1969 he founded the AREA (Atelier de Recherche et d'Etudes en Aménagement), an interdisciplinary team which gained widespread acclaim in the 1970s after winning several contests organized by the new towns. Sarfati trained at the Ecole

Nationale Supérieure des Beaux-Arts, the Tony Garnier Cursus and the Paris Institute of Town Planning. He is a professor and workshop-director at the Paris-Conflans School of Architecture, and also holds posts at the Ministry of Equipment, Department of Architecture (architect/advisor) and at the National Council of Architects where he is Vice-President. Recent projects include competition entries for two phases of construction for the Grand Stade at Saint-Denis; redevelopment of the Augustusplatz in Leipzig; reconstruction of the Saint-Exupéry grammar school in Créteil, and redevelopment of departmental archives, Châteauroux.

Martha Schwartz Inc., 167 Pemberton Street, Cambridge, Massachusetts 02140, USA Martha Schwartz studied at the University of Michigan (Bachelor of Fine Arts, 1973, and Master of Landscape Architecture, 1976) and at the Harvard University Graduate School of Design (Landscape Architecture Programme). She worked for the SWA Group before going into partnership, first with Peter Walker and later with Ken Smith and David Meyer. She founded her own practice in 1990 which specializes in unique landscape design and site-specific public art commissions. Her aim of relating landscape to art and culture has been applied to schemes ranging from public spaces to private residential gardens, and from public plazas and parks to mixed-use developments. Projects include a roof garden for the Center for Innovative Technology, Fairfax, Virginia; the redesign of a glass-covered interior street for Becton Dickinson Immunocytrometry Division, San Jose, California; the plaza forecourt at the Ahmanson Theater, Los Angeles; California College of Arts and Crafts masterplan study; schematic design for vehicular and pedestrian circulation at the Greater Buffalo International Airport; masterplan studies for an art park and surrounding streetscale at the Bass Museum of Art, Miami Beach, Florida; and various parks throughout the United States, as well as commissioned artworks and private residences. The practice is currently working on the masterplan for a public park and nine-block area, and landscape design services for the International Jazz Hall of Fame, Kansas City, and the Baltimore Inner Harbor project (arising from a competition win to develop Baltimore's growing Inner Harbor area). Martha Schwartz's work has been published extensively and in 1991 she was awarded both Honor and Merit Awards from the American Society of Landscape Architects for The Citadel Grand Allée, Commerce, California and the Becton Dickinson atrium respectively. She is visiting critic and Adjunct Professor of Landscape Architecture at the Harvard University Graduate School of Design.

Shodo Suzuki, Suzuki Landscape Architect & Associates, H2 Building 2F, 3-9-8 Minami-Ikebukuro, Toshima-ku, Tokyo 171, Japan
Shodo Suzuki established Suzuki Landscape Architect & Associates in 1974. He studied at Chiba University where he received a Bachelor of Engineering degree in Horticulture in 1960. Before founding his own practice, he worked for Ashihara Architect and Associates as well as serving on the Tokyo Olympic Games Committee. Projects include the Garden of the Sheraton Grande Tokyo Bay Hotel; the Shin-Kawasaki Intelligent City Plaza in the Sanbonmatsu Royal Hotel Garden; the garden of the Koga City Folk Museum and the exterior of Toyosu ON Building, garden of the Marumine Kanko Hotel. His work has been published widely within Japan and has received national prizes, including the Japan Society of Landscape Gardeners Award for a series of works based on research into the principles of garden construction. Suzuki has lectured at Harvard University (1989), at the First International Garden Festival in France (1992) and at Tokyo National University of Fine Arts and Music (1993).

Tract (WA) Pty Ltd, 48 King Street, Perth, Western Australia 6000 Tract is a leading professional consulting firm providing services in planning design, urban design, environmental analysis and landscape architecture. Associated operations in Melbourne, Sydney and Brisbane enable the firm to call upon a wide range of national and international experience. Work includes landscape architecture schemes such as the Joondalup Estate Public Open Spaces and Central Park, Perth, the Northern Rail Link Stations and the Bus Junction Roof Garden. Recently completed urban design schemes include the Jull Street Mall, Armadale, the Mends Street Redevelopment, and the South and East Perth development projects. Over the past ten years Tract's involvement in public art has increased and it now uses this as an integral part of community projects. Recent state and national design awards number Civic Design Prizes in 1993 and 1994 for work completed on the Joondalup Central Park and the Jull Street Mall; the AILA National Project Award (1994) for Joondalup; and the Landscape Irrigation and Nursery Awards (1995) for the East Perth Redevelopment.

Michael Van Valkenburgh Associates, 231 Concord Avenue, Cambridge, Massachusetts 02138, USA Michael Van Valkenburgh Associates has directed the design and construction of over 200 landscapes for institutional, public and private clients across the United States and in Canada, France and Korea. Recent work includes the design of Mill Race Park, Columbus, Indiana; the masterplan and design for the renovation of Harvard Yard for Harvard University, and the Walker Art Center Sculpture Garden for the Minneapolis Park and Recreation Board. Michael Van Valkenburgh trained at the Cornell University College of Agriculture and at the University of Illinois where he obtained a Master's degree in Landscape Architecture in 1977. He was a 1988 Advanced Design Fellow of the American Academy of Rome and is Chairman of the Department of Landscape Architecture at the Harvard University Graduate School of Design. Van Valkenburgh currently teaches at Harvard where he is Professor of Landscape Architecture, and has recently had a monograph published by Princeton Architectural Press. He has been honoured for his work, receiving the Planning and Urban Design Merit Award (1993) from the American Society of Landscape Architects for Harvard Yard Masterplan, which also took the Honor Award from the National Trust for Historic Preservation (1994) and, along with Mill Race Park, the Honor Award from the Boston Society of Landscape Architects (1993).

Peter Walker, William Johnson and Partners, 739 Allston Way, Berkeley, California 94710, USA
The office of Peter Walker, William Johnson and Partners was formed in 1983. Its aim is to challenge traditional concepts of landscape design and this attitude has been applied to a variety of projects within the United States, ranging from private residential gardens and parks to hotels, plazas, campuses, large-scale corporate headquarters, mixed-use developments and new communities. The firm has participated successfully in many design competitions, including the redesign of the historic Todos Santos Plaza, Concord, California; the Marina Linear Park in San Diego, and the Performing Arts Center in Fremont, California. In 1992 the firm merged with William J. Johnson Associates, a practice which concentrates on campus planning, community revitalization, public workshop facilitation, urban design, waterfront and environmental studies, historic preservation, planning, graphic communications and computer technology. Recent or soon to be completed projects include the Principal Mutual Life Insurance Company Corporate Expansion, Iowa (1996); the Countryside Landfill in Grayslake, Illinois; the Oyama Training Centre in Tochigi Prefecture, Japan (1995); the University of California San Diego Library Walk (1995); the Toyota Municipal Museum of Art, Aichi Prefecture, Japan (1995); the Kempinski Hotel, Munich, and the Martin Luther King Promenade, Civic Pond and Park, San Diego (1996). Peter Walker has served as a consultant and advisor to a number of public agencies and institutions such as the Redevelopment Agency of San Francisco. He is the former chairman of the Department of Landscape Architecture and acting director of the Urban Design Programme at the Harvard University Graduate School of Design. He is a Fellow of both the American Society of Landscape Architects and the Urban Land Institute. William Johnson is President of the Landscape Architecture Foundation, Fellow of the American Society of Landscape Architects and Professor Emeritus at the University of Michigan.

West 8 Landscape Architects Ltd, Rijnhaven nz 22, P.O. Box 24326, 3007 DH, Rotterdam, The Netherlands The Rotterdam-based practice of West 8 is an international team of 15 architects, landscape designers, town planners and industrial designers led by the landscape architect Adriaan Geuze. Projects include the Shell Project, Oosterschelde, Schiphol Airport, Amsterdam, and the street market in Binnenrotten.

Robin Winogrond, Feuerbacher Heide 16, D-70192 Stuttgart, Germany Robin Winogrond studied at the University of Wisconsin where she received a Bachelor of Arts degree in Environmental Design in 1979. She went on to undertake post-graduate studies at the San Francisco Center for Architecture and Urban Design and a marble sculpture course in Cortona, Italy. She obtained a Master of Landscape Architecture from the Louisiana State University and was Artist in Residence at the Staatliche Akademie der Bildenden Kunste in Stuttgart from 1989 to 1990. She worked for Camiros Ltd, Child Associates, and Richard Burck and Associates before becoming a freelance landscape architect in 1989. Robin Winogrond is a Member of the Chamber of Architects in Baden Württemberg, Assistant Professor at the University of Stuttgart and has been Guest Professor of Landscape Architecture at the University of Agricultural Sciences, Vienna (March 1996 to July 1996).

Zen Environmental Design, Yomiuri Fukuoka Bldg 7F, 1-12-15 Akasaka, Chuo-ku, Fukuoka-shi, Japan Zen Environmental Design was founded in 1959 and is involved in many aspects of environmental design, from large-scale city planning and the landscape architecture of resorts and parks, to street furniture and sign design. It has won both national and international acclaim for its work and has recently started to increase the number of overseas projects undertaken. Major clients include the Japanese Government, Ministry of Construction; Prefectural offices; the Seibu Saison Group; Misui Real Estate; the Japan Railroad Company and the Daiei Group (Twin Dome City Company).

Credits

1.1 Landscape Park Duisburg Nord (part of the International Construction Exhibition Emscherpark), Duisburg-Meiderich, Ruhr Area, Germany

Landscape architect: Latz + Partner. Project designer: Prof. Peter Latz. Collaborators: Karlheinz Danielzik, Alexander Kuhn, Tilman Latz, Stefanie Meinicke, Christine Rupp-Stoppel, Martina Schneider, Peter Wilde. Co-architect: G. Lipkowski. Client: Landesentwicklungs Gesellschaft Nordrhein-Westfalen. Building supervisor: Latz/Riehl. Co-operating community groups: Gartenamt Stadt Duisburg; Gesellschaft für Industriekultur; IG Nordpark; IBA (International Construction Exhibition). Landscape consultants: Trautmann GmbH, Werner Ewertz, Langenfurth, Lohbeck GmbH, Lankes GmbH, K.W. Peters GmbH, Walbrodt u Böllhoff. Steel construction: Rolf Hüsken, RAM GmbH. Concrete sawing works: Bohrtechnik Westerwald GmbH. Sealing: Stutz Nachf. GmbH.

1.2 Emscher Landscape Park, River Emscher Valley, Rheinland-Westfalen, Germany

Landscape co-ordinator: IBA Emscher Park. Client: Land North-Rhine/Westphalia and Local Authorities of Duisburg, Oberhausen, Mülheim an der Ruhr, Bottrop, Essen, Gladbeck, Bochum, Gelsenkirchen, Recklinghausen, Herne, Herten, Castrop-Rauxel, Waltrop, Lünen, Dortmund, Kamen and Bergkamen. General director: Prof. Karl Ganser. Consultant/selector: Minister of Urban Development and Transport of North-Rhine/Westphalia. Masterplanning: Kommunalverband Ruhrgebiet. Finance: Emscher-Lippe Ecology Programme.

1.3 Bürgerpark auf der Hafeninsel, Saarbrücken, Germany

Landscape architect: Latz & Partner. Project team: Gunter Bartholmai, Nikki Biegler, Hanno Dutt, Rüdiger Haase, Gerd Hegelmann, Anneliese Latz, Hans Georg Ohlmeier, Christine Rupp, Ines Schulz, Monika Stahr. Client: Town of Saarbrücken, Town Planning Department. Collaborating community groups: Baudezernat (surveyor), Tiefbauamt (underground workings); Gartenamt (forestry); employment agencies. Steel and girder construction: G. Becker GmbH,

B. Schönenberger, Fr Wolff. Road construction and paving, masonry: E. Roberts, Lothar Daub, MNS, J.C. Dittgen. Iron, concrete construction and masonry: Hans Hanus GmbH. Excavations, drainage and pond: J.C. Dittgen. Suppliers: E. Roberts, Müller-Platz (plants); DZ – Licht (lighting); Runge GmbH (manufactured benches); L & B (new clinkers).

1.4 Byxbee Landfill Park, Palo Alto, California, USA

Landscape architect: Hargreaves Associates. Client: City of Palo Alto. General contractor: Granite Construction. Artists: Peter Richards, Michel Oppenheimer.

1.5 Ecomusée, Ungersheim, Alsace, France

Landscape architect: EDAW Jarvis France Sarl. Client: Ecomusée, Ungersheim, Alsace, France. Architect and gardeners: Ecomusée personnel. Museum design specialists: Musées sans Frontiers. Nature conservancy: Conservatoire des Sites Naturels D'Alsace.

1.6 The Lakeside Gardens, Garden Festival, Ebbw Vale, Wales, UK

Landscape architect: Eachus Huckson Landscape Architects Ltd. Client: Garden Festival Wales Ltd. Architect: Brown & Parnaby. Main contractor: Brunswick Contractors Ltd. Engineer: Ove Arup & Partners. Quantity surveyor: Tweeds. Soft landscape contractor: Brophy Plc.

1.7 Grand Allée of The Citadel, City of Commerce, California, USA

Landscape architect: Schwartz/Smith/Meyer Inc. Project team: Martha Schwartz, Ken Smith, David Meyer. Client: Trammell Crow Company. General contractor: HCB Contractors. Landscape contractor: Tracy & Ryder. Principal architect: The Nadel Partnership. Retail architect: Sussman/Prejza. Irrigation: ISC Group.

1.8 White River State Park (not built)

Landscape architect: Rundell Ernstberger Associates. Project team: Eric Fulford (associate); Eric Ernstberger (principal); Kevin Osburn (designer). Client: White River State Park Commission/State of Indiana. Architect: Callahan Associates; Able Ringham Moake Park. Illustrator: Eric Schleef Illustration. Collaborator: Museum Indiana Council of Advisors.

2.1 Louisiana Museum of Art – The Lake Garden (and the Children's House), Gl. Strandvej, DK 3050 Humlebaek, Denmark

Landscape architect: Lea Nørgaard & Vibeke Holscher. Client: Louisiana Museum. Main

contractor: K.Fl. Jacobsen. Subcontractors: Richard Juul (woodwork); Michael Pederson (resident gardener). Consulting engineer: Carl Bro, Balslev Consulting Engineers. Land artist: Alfio Bonanno. Willow wickerwork: Dansk Pileavl. Louisiana Museum collaborators: Knud W. Jensen, Torben Jensen.

2.2 Hellings Street Play Area, Wapping, London, UK

Landscape architect: Kinnear Landscape Architects. Client: London Docklands Development Corporation. Main contractor: T. Loughman and Company Ltd. Structural engineer: Techniker. Quantity surveyor: Yeoman and Edwards. Artist: Susie Kinnear.

2.3 Kindergarten (Children's Playground) Birken III, Marktheidenfeld, Germany

Landscape architect: Robin Winogrond. Architect and site supervision: Willi Müller. Garden and landscape construction: Peter Kuhn. Carpenter: Keller Woodworks. Fountain: Kettner Fountain Co. Industrial designer: Mathias Burhenne. Technical consultation: Klaus Lohman.

2.4 Himeji Mitate Park, Himeji City, Hyogo, Japan

Landscape architect: Mitsuru Man Senda, Environment Design Institute. Client: Takara Planning Co. Main contractor: Okabe Co. Landscape contractor: Koho Construction Co.

2.5 Kromhoutpark, Tilburg, The Netherlands

Landscape architect: Bureau B + B. Project team: Bart Brands, Michael van Gessel, Jos Jacobs (project architects); Francien van Kempen, Rob Lubrecht, Karen Reddering. Computer visualization: Thierry Labbé. Client: City of Tilburg. Construction consultant: Adviesbureau Markslag b.v. Vegetation consultant: Charley Younge. Playground facilities: Speelhart b.v; Velopa. Electric installation: Jacobs-Electro. Implementation: Oranjewoud.

2.6 Weesner Family Amphitheater, Apple Valley, Minnesota, USA

Landscape architect: Hammel Green and Abrahamson Inc. Project designer: Thomas Oslund. Client: Minnesota Zoological Gardens. General contractor: Arkay Construction. Architects: Bill Blanski, Jim Butler. Landscape consultant: Randy Lueth. Structural engineer: Tony Staeger. Acoustical consultant: STI Inc. Stone: Mankato Kasota Stone,Inc. Metal structure: White Oak Metals. Benches: Structural Wood Corporation. Canopy fabric: Boadair Inc. Native and wetland vegetation: Prairie Restoration,Inc.

2.7 Parc Terrasson-la-Villedieu, Dordogne , France

Landscape architect: Kathryn Gustafson. Project team: K. Gustafson, Anton James, Philippe Marchand, Sylvie Farges. Client: City of Terrasson. Architect: Ian Ritchie Architects. Landscape: Moser. Stone supplier: Rossi. Stone installation: Audeguil. Glass roof: Glasbau Steele. Metal works: Magimel/Pommarel. Gate artist: Peter Forakis.

2.8 Schlosspark, Grevenbroich, Nordrhein-Westfalen, Germany

Landscape architect: Georg Penker, Landschaftsarchitekt. Project team: Christoph Gerdes, Annette Demmer, Claus Thiele, Agus Vincentius, Ellen Förster. Client: Landesgartenschau Grevenbroich 1995 GmbH. Main contractor: Firma Leisten GmbH und Co.KG. Project manager: Thomas Wündrich. Planting consultant: Rainer Lechner Neuss. Hydraulic engineer: Rademacher & Partner. Art concept: Ian Hamilton Finlay. Lamps: Siemens. Concrete: Fiege & Bertoli.

2.9 Bryant Park, Manhattan, New York, USA

Landscape architect: Hanna/Olin Ltd, Landscape Architecture, Urban Design. Client: Bryant Park Restoration Corporation. General contractor: LaStrada General Contracting Corporation. Construction manager: Tishman Construction Corporation of New York. Consultants: H.M. Brandston & Partners (lighting design); Joseph R. Loring (site, civil/electrical and mechanical engineer); Robert R. Rosenwasser (structural engineer). Perennial planting: Lynden B. Miller – Garden Design.

2.10 Niigata Prefecture Museum of Modern Art, Nagaoka City, Niigata Prefecture, Japan

Landscape architect: Shunmyo Masuno of Japan Landscape Consultants. Client: Niigata Prefecture. Main contractor: Taisei Corporation. Collaborating architect: Nikon Sekkei.

2.11/2.14 Parc de Catalunya, Sabadell, Barcelona, Spain/Parc Nus de la Trinitat, Barcelona, Spain

Landscape architects: Enric Batlle, Joan Roig. Project team: Enric Batlle, Joan Roig (principal architects); Lluis Roig (architects' assistant); Pere Largo, Gerardo Rodriguez (engineering collaborators); Teresa Gali, Manel Colominas (landscape collaborators); Lluis Jubert, Luis Maldonado (assistants); Nael Colomines (agronomist); Joan Ramon Clasca (engineer). Client (Catalunya): I.D.E.M.S. (Institute for the Development of the Eix Macia) Sabadell Council. Client (Trinitat): I.M.P.U.S.A. (Municipal Institute for Urban Development). Street furniture: Santa & Cole.

2.12 Parc del Litoral, Olympic Village, Barcelona, Spain

Landscape architect: MBM Arquitectes. Project team: Josep Martorell, Oriol Bohigas, David Mackay, Albert Puigdomènech. Clients: Vila Olimpica S.A., HOLSA (Holding Olympic S.A.), MOPTMA (Ministerio de Obras Publicas, Transportes y Medio Ambiente). Co-ordinating architect: Liliana Antoniucci. Architects: Nicklas Dünebacke, Hortensia Palou, Oriol Capdevila. Sculpture: Auke de Bries, Antoni Llena, Antoni Rosselló. Sculpture design: Xavier Mariscal. Technical officer: José A. Torroja. Urbanization: IOC. Technical advisor, Barcelona City Council: Albert Camps. Industrial designer: Ramón Mulet. Construction: Cubiertas y MZOV S.A. Consultants: CAMUNSA, IDOM, INYPESA.

2.13 International Horticultural Exhibition Floriade, The Hague-Zoetermeer, The Netherlands

Landscape architect: DENruijter.etc. Project designer: Gert Koning. Clients: The National Horticultural Council; Municipalities of Zoetermeer and The Hague. Urban designer: Tom Hinse. Engineer: Cees de Vrieze. Main contractor: Seignette.

2.15 Uppermill Cemetery, Saddleworth, Yorkshire, UK

Landscape architect: Robert Camlin. Client: Saddleworth Parish Council, Uppermill. Stone walling and planting: Pennine Heritage.

3.1 Shell Project, Oosterschelde Estuary, Zeeland, The Netherlands

Landscape architect: West 8 Landscape Architects Ltd. Clients: Ministry of Waterways and Public Works (Rijkswaterstaat), Provincial Board of Zeeland.

3.2 Parque Ecologico Xochimilco, Mexico City, Mexico

Landscape architect: Grupo de Diseño Urbano Project team: Mario Schjetnan, José Luis Pérez. Clients: Delegacion Xochimilco; Departamento del Distrito Federal. Direction and co-ordination: Borough of Xochimilco, Construction: Department of Hydraulic Resources, Mexico City; Public Works Department, Mexico City. Historical research and excavations: Instituto Nacional de Antropologia e Historia, National University of Mexico. Irrigation systems: Garza Maldonado y Asociados. Electrical engineering: R.C.L. Ingenieros. Botanical consultant: Dr Alejandro Novelo. Graphic design: Ricardo Albin, Alfonso Liceaga.

3.3 Joondalup Central Park, Joondalup, Perth, Western Australia

Landscape architect: Tract (WA) Pty Ltd. Client: Landcorp. Collaborating landscape designer: Chris Dance. Soft landscape: Environmental Industries. Engineer: G.B. Hill. Civil engineer: Ertech. Electrical engineer: ETC P/C. Irrigation: Hydro Plan. Artists: David Woodland (Woodland Studios), Leon Pereclis, Wendy Herrington. Granite: Silk Road P/C. Limestone, timber: Bunnings.

3.4 Seven Spirit Wilderness, Coral Bay, Cobourg Peninsula, Arnhem Land, Northern Territory, Australia

Landscape architect: EcoSystems. Designer: David Metcalfe. Client: Cobourg Peninsula Sanctuary Board. Main contractor: Barclay Mowlem. Landscape contractor: Darwin Plant Wholesalers. Mechanical and electrical engineer: MGF Consultants. Architect: MLE & D. Civil engineer, structural engineer and services consultant: Acer Vaughan. Lighting consultant: MGF Consultants.

3.5 Center for Regenerative Studies, Pomona, California, USA

Landscape architects: John Lyle, Ronald Izumita. Client: California State Polytechnic University. Landscape construction manager: Steven Nawrath. Design development and construction documents: Betsey Dougherty. Landscape construction and planting: Center residents.

3.6 The Taung Monument, Bophuthatswana National Parks Board, North West Province, South Africa

Landscape architect: Environmental Design Partnership (Pty) Ltd. Project team: Gareth Singleton, Sarah Singleton (directors-in-charge); Keith Rowe (resident landscape architect). Client: Bophuthatswana National Parks Board. Main contractor: Environmental Design Partnership. Subcontractors: Top Turf Irrigation (irrigation); Hydro seeding (Hydromulch); Sentinel Fencing Systems (fencing). Interpretive planner: Phoebe McCleod. Archaeologist and interpretive planner: Colin Campbell. Consulting civil, structural, mechanical and electrical engineer: Edwards, Van Vuuren and Zborowski. Anthropologist: Dr Jeff McKee, University of the Witwatersrand. Buxton mine manager and later technical director: Brian Lowther, Pretoria Portland Cement.

3.7 Ibaraki Nature Museum/Park, Iwai City, Ibaraki, Japan

Landscape architect and architect: Mitsuru Man Senda, Environment Design Institute. Client: Ibaraki Prefecture. Main contractors: Okabe Co. (play facilities); Kotobuki Co. Structure: Kozo Keikaku Kenkyusho, Construction Planning Institute. Equipment: Building Equipment Design Institute. Lighting: TL Yamigiwa Institute. Signage: Kojima Ryouhei Design Office. Construction: Taisei/Mutou/Shouei joint venture; Obayashi/

Nissan/Shouyaku joint venture. Electricity: Wako/ Sanko joint Venture; Rokko/Kyowa joint venture.

3.8 Mount St Helens National Volcanic Monument, Gifford Pinchot National Forest, Washington State, USA

Landscape architect and consultant: EDAW. Project manager and lead designer: Charles Morris Anderson. Construction documents: Stephen Ray. Client: US Department of Agriculture, Forest Service. Prime consultant: Spencer Associates (architecture and planning). Consultant: KCM Engineers. Interpretive designer: Barry Howard.

3.9 Milton Country Park, Cambridgeshire, UK

Landscape architect: Landscape Design Associates. Project team: Tony Leadley (project director); Prof. Robert Tregay (partner); David Thompson (senior landscape architect). Client: South Cambridgeshire District Council. Contractors: Foxglove Contracting Ltd (reclamation); Tilhill Landscapes (phases 1 and 2); Worboys & Winter Landscapes (phase 3). Visitor centre, toilet block and car-park: South Cambridgeshire District Council's Architects. Floating sculpture: Peter Fluck. VE Day memorial: David Kindersley Workshop.

3.10 Berjaya Langkawi Beach Resort Sdn Bhd, Burau Bay, Langkawi Island, Malaysia

Landscape architect and site planning consultant: Aspinwall Clouston. Project team: Robbert Van Nouhuys (project director); Henry Steed (consultant); David Martin (senior landscape architect); Ludovic Devriendt, Devendiran S.T. Mani, Eric Ye Lee Tsen (project landscape architects); Mohammad Hasni Bin Hassan (project technician); Roslina Binti Ahmad, Norliah Binti Abdul Wahid (assistant landscape architects). Site team: David Martin, Lars Pertwee, Scott Sawyer (resident landscape architects). Client: Berjaya Langkawi Resort. Main contractor: Bridgecon Engineering. Soft landscape subcontractor: Bakti Jelata Sdn Bhd. Architect: Akitek Daya Reka. Civil and structural engineers: Syed Muhammad, Hooi and Binnie Sdn Bhd. Electrical engineer: Mektricon Sdn Bhd. Quantity surveyor: JUBC. External light consultants: Light Sound Image Systems. Timber work and purpose-made aluminium castings: Intouch Design. Signage supplier: Wilayah Enterprises Sdn Bhd. External pavilions and shelters: Masri Basirah Construction and Landscape. Artificial rockwork: Rock Art Sdn Bhd.

4.1 Pershing Square, Los Angeles, California, USA

Architect: Legorreta Arquitectos. Project team: Ricardo Legorreta, Noé Castro, Victor Legorreta, Gerardo Alonso. Landscape architect: Hanna/Olin Ltd. Project designer: Laurie Olin. Clients: Pershing Square Property Owners and the Los Angeles Community Redevelopment Agency. Main contractor: Turner Construction. Executive architect: Langdon Wilson Architecture Planning. Co-ordination: Maguire Thomas Partners. Structural design: Nabith Yussef & Associates. Civil engineer: Psomas Associates. Lighting consultant: Lighting Design Alliance. Fountain consultant: Waterscape Technology Incorporated. Construction manager: Turner Construction. Artist: Barbara McCarren.

4.2 Iki-Iki Plaza, 12 Ichiban-cho, Chiyoda-ku, Tokyo, Japan

Landscape architect: Suzuki Landscape Architect & Associates. Project designer: Shodo Suzuki. Main contractor: Taisei, Sato, Tekken Construction J.V. (Architecture). Subcontractor: Mitsui-Bussan Forestry Co. Ltd, Shinsei Construction Corporation (stonework); Fuji-Ueki Corporation (planting work). Architect: Chiyoda Ward Office, Okuno Architects & Engineers.

4.3 Ole Bulls Plass, Bergen, Norway

Landscape architect: Arkitektgruppen Cubus. Project team: Ingrid Haukeland (landscape architect); Axel Somme (urban designer); Arne Saelen. Client: City of Bergen. Main contractor: Anleggsgartnermester NAML Rolf Vaglid. Subcontractor: Anleggsgartnermester NAML Jan I Askeland. Granite slabs: Jogra; Skiferindustri. Stone carving: Rablokk & Naturstein; Eikner Naturstein. Cast iron: Furnes-Hamjern NCC. Wrought iron: Sveis & Mekanisk industri; Ingenior Christen Smith; Einar Olsen. Adhesives: Betomur. Street lights, traffic signs and litter-bins: Orsta Stalindustri. Lighting: BEGA c/o AKB. Concrete: NOBI-Haugland. Sculptor: Asbjörn Andresen.

4.4 Place Charles de Gaulle, Vichy, France

Landscape architect: Latitude Nord. Project team: Gilles Vexlard, Laurence Vacherot. Client: City of Vichy. Main contractor: Jean Lefebvre. Structure: Arcora. Light concept: Concepto – R. Narboni. Artist: J. Marc Bourry. Fountain: G.F.C. (stonework); Rockdall (facing); Bornhauser Molinari (waterworks). Kiosk and stacks: G.F.C. (civil engineer); Rockdall (facing); S.A.E.B. (glass structure). Planting: Treyve, Laquet, Jardinan. Street furniture: Sarragala.

4.5 Chuo Plaza in Momochi Seaside Park, 2 Momochihama, Sawara-ku, Fukuoka City, Japan

Landscape architect: Zen Environmental Design Project team: Kyuji Nakamura, Katsumi Nakayama. Special thanks to Yodogawa, Yoshika, Tokunaga. Client: Port and Harbour Bureau, Fukuoka City. Masterplan: Jun Architectural Regional-Planning Consultants Office. Architect: M.A.Y. Architects Office. Engineering design: Setsubi Sogo Keikaku Inc. Culvert bridge for expressway: Toa Kensetsu Gijutsu Inc. Consultants: Fukuoka City Expressway Momochi Area Structural Investigation Committee; Professors of Fukuoka City Urban Beautification Committee; TL Yamagiwa Laboratory Inc. (lighting). Architecture: Samejimagumi Inc. Fire prevention : Nishihara Company. Mechanical service: Itakura Industry Inc. Electric installation: Taiyo & Miyazaki joint venture. Gardening: Aiko & Sokaku joint venture (1994); Nakamura Ryokuchi Landscape Construction Inc. (1995).

4.6 JT Building, Toranomon, Minato-ku, Tokyo, Japan

Landscape architect and architect: Nikken Sekkei Ltd. Project designer: Masanori Nishida. Project team: Hiroshi Ibe (project manager); Tadao Kamei (project architect); Hideyuki Sato, Taisuke Inoue (architects); Mitsugu Asano (structural engineer); Hiroshi Miyahara (electrical engineer); Noriaki Kitamura (mechanical engineer); Masanori Nishida (landscape design). Client: Japan Tobacco Inc. Main contractors: Taisei Corporation, Kajima Corporation, Toda Corporation. Lighting consultant: TL Yamagiwa Laboratory Inc. Main artists: Kenneth Snelson, Marta Pan, Sheila Hicks, Toshihiro Katayama.

4.7 The Belvedere, Battery Park City, New York, USA

Landscape architect: Child Associates. Architect: Mitchell/Giurgola Architects. Project team for Child Associates: Susan Child (principal-in-charge); Robert Corning (project landscape architect); John Grove, Douglas Reed, Anita Berrizbeitia. Project team for Mitchell/Giurgola Architects: Steven M. Goldberg (principal-in-charge); John Kurtz (project principal); Stuart Crawford (project architect); Niall Cain, Carol Loewenson. Client: Battery Park City Authority. Construction manager: Raytheon Engineers and Constructors. Engineers: Weidlinger Associates (structural); Lehr Associates (mechanical/electrical). Lighting consultant: H.M. Brandston & Partners. Artist: Martin Puryear (pylons). Landscape contractor: Steven Dubner Landscaping Inc. General contractor: Sette Juliano/LandSite joint venture. Pylons: Metal Forms Inc. Electrical contractor: 99 Commerce Electric. Granite: Pansini Stone. Wall railings and handrails: Epic Contracting Corporation. Esplanade railings: Royal Guard Fence Company.

4.8 Ma Hang Village, Ma Hang Valley, Stanley, Hong Kong

Landscape architect: Stephanie Crockett, Landscape Group, Hong Kong Housing Authority.

Project team: Stephanie Crockett; Dennis Ko (chief architect); Penny Ward (initial chief architect); John Lambon (senior architect); Kevin Yeung (architect); Rosman Wai (initial architect). Client: Housing Department – New Development Branch. Building contractor: Hsin Chong. Artificial rock: Asia Rock Art. Planting contractor: Bluet Garden. Colour consultation: Michel Cler. Play equipment: Claridge House (Gametime).

4.9 Beethovenpark, Cologne, Germany

Landscape architect: Bödeker, Wagenfeld & Partner. Project team: Richard Bödeker, Horst Wagenfeld, Klaus Steinhauer, Jörg Weisser, Thomas Fenner, Mrs Schnittka, Mr Schomakers, Mr Kampfer. Client and building contractor: Gerling Konzern. Architect: Hentrich-Petschnigg & Partner, BDA. Project partners: dt8-Planungsgruppe. Landscape contractors: Kurt Papsdorf (hard landscape); Hoemann GmbH (soft landscape). Architectural contractor: Hochtief AG. Suppliers: Fiege + Bertoli GmbH & Co. KG, Heinrich Klostermann GmbH & Co. KG (paving material); Ing. Holzbau Brückenbau (wooden terraces and bridges); Springbrunnenbau (fountain technology); Joh. Bruns Deutsche Exportbaumschulen (supplying nursery).

4.10 Binnenrotte Marketplein, Rotterdam, The Netherlands

Landscape architect: West 8 Landscape Architects Ltd. Client: The Metropolitan Service of Urban Planning and Public Housing. Main contractor: KWS. Technical realization: Engineering office of road construction and green planning, Rotterdam Public Works Department. Light masts: Kaal. Bicycle shelter: B & G. Concrete paving: Blyeco Concrete. Anti-parking rail: De Boer Steel and Concrete. Litter-bins and benches: Verwo Concrete.

4.11 Rue de la République, Lyons, France

Landscape architect: Alain Sarfati–AREA. Project team: Alain Sarfati, Nathalie Bara. Collaborators: BREA; Bureau d'études et maître d'oeuvre VRD. Client: Grand Lyon. Lighting consultants: CIEL, Pierre Bideau. Groundwork: De Filipis, Monin, Gauthey, Maïa-Saunier. Coating: SCREG. Asphalt: SMAC. Lighting: Sud-Est. Grilles: SGMS. Granite: Clolus SA (Bleu de Lanhelin); Ferymag SA (Blanc de Berrocal). Fountain: Petavit, ATF; SOGEA. Light fittings: Mazda, Lenzi, Wilmotte. Luminescent diodes: LEC.

5.1 Prospect Green, Sacramento Valley, California, USA

Landscape architect: Hargreaves Associates. General contractor: Hensel Phelps Construction. Landscape contractor: Aerco Pacific.

5.2 50 Avenue Montaigne Courtyard, Avenue Montaigne, Paris, France

Landscape architect: Michael Van Valkenburgh Associates. Client: SNC 50 Avenue Montaigne. Architect: Olivier Vidal (office building); Kohn Pedersen Fox (interior design). General contractor: Dumez il de France. Construction manager: Coteba Managements. Landscape contractor: A. Cantin et fils. Water columns: Etm Voisin. Stonework: L'Européene dé Marbre. Structural engineer: Ocmulgee Associates. Lighting consultant: Jerry Kugler Associates. Benches: Judy McKee. Plants: Pépinières Guillot-Bourne. Lighting fixtures: Nightscaping.

5.3 Plaza Tower, 600 Anton Boulevard, Costa Mesa, California, USA

Landscape architect: Peter Walker, William Johnson and Partners. Project team: Doug Findlay, Tom Leader, Tony Sinkosky, John Threadgill, Hiko Mitani. Clients: 600 Anton Boulevard Associates, IBM Corporation, C.J. Segerstrom and Sons. General contractor: Peck/Jones. Landscape contractor: Tracy and Ryder Landscape Inc. Architecture: Cesar Pelli and Associates, CRS Sirrine Inc. Structural engineer: Johnson and Nielsen Associates. Civil engineer: The Keith Companies. Fountain mechanical and electrical consultant: Fountain Tech Company. Irrigation: I.S.C. Group Inc. Sculpture: Aiko Miyawaki Isozaki. Concrete unit pavers: Euro America Inc. Integral concrete colour: L.M. Scofield and Co. Textured stainless steel: Ardmore Textured Metals Inc. Stainless steel band fabrication: Corona Aluminium Company. Granite pavers: Raymond Granite/Cold Springs Granite Co. Fountains: Rock and Waterscape Inc. Fountain and sculpture lights: Hydrel. Precast concrete pots: Dura Art Stone. Soil amendments: Gro Power Inc.

5.4 Centre for Advanced Science and Technology, Harima Science Garden City, Kamigouri-town, Hyogo Prefecture, Japan

Landscape architect: Peter Walker, William Johnson and Partners. Collaborator: Heads Company Ltd. Client: Hyogo Prefecture. Architects: Arata Isozaki & Associates, ADH Architects. General contractors: Takenaka, Arai, Kitamura. Landscape contractor: Hanshin Engel, Namura Landscape. Stonework: Daishin Shosi. Signage: File. Lighting design: Lighting Planners Associates.

5.5 National Research Institute for Metals, Science and Technology, Tsukuba City, Ibaraki Prefecture, Japan

Landscape architect: Shunmyo Masuno of Japan Landscape Consultants. Client: Metals, Science and Technology Agency. Main contractor: Hazama Corporation. Collaborating architect: Nihon Sekkei + RIA.

5.6 Forum Bonn, Bonn, Germany

Landscape architect: Bödeker, Wagenfeld & Partner. Project team: Richard Bödeker, Horst Wagenfeld, Klaus Steinhauer, Bernhard Schwering. Client: Moderne Stadt. Supervision: Hans Kampfer. Architect: Hentrich, Petschnigg & Partner. Landscape contractors: Kurt Papsdorf (hard landscape); Hoemann GmbH (soft landscape). Lighting consultant: Kress + Adams. Structural engineer: Wolfgang Naumann. Suppliers: Heinz Alfs GmbH (natural stone); Joh. Bruns (supplying nursery); Vannuci Piante Azienda Agricola (*Magnolia grandiflora* Solitärs); KSP Ingenieurgesellschaft mbh (building equipment).

5.7 Outdoor Design for the Research and Development Centre of the Heidelberger Druckmaschinen AG, Heidelberg, Germany

Landscape architect: Georg Penker, Landschaftsarchitekt. Client: Heidelberger Druckmaschinen AG. Architect: Hentrich-Petschnigg & Partner. Landscape manager: Garten und Landschaftsbau GmbH & Co. KG. Automatic irrigation: Optima-System.

5.8 Shell Headquarters, Rueil, Paris, France

Landscape architect: Kathryn Gustafson. Landscape: Moser. Stone and installation: Rossi. Glass structure engineer: Henry Bardsley.

5.9 Genentech Founders Research Center (FRC), San Francisco, California, USA

Landscape architect: MPA Design. Project team: Michael Painter, David W. Nelson. Client: Genentech Corporation administered by SRG Partnership Architects. General contractor: Rudolph & Sletten Inc. Landscape contractor: Shooter & Butts. Building architect: SRG Partnership. Irrigation consultant: Brookwater Design. Electrical consultant: Affiliated Engineers Inc. Civil engineer: Brian Kangas Foulk. Pavers: Hanover Architectural Products. Slate paving: Burlington Slate Ltd. Benches, chairs and tables: Forms and Surfaces. Irrigation equipment: Rainbird.

5.10 Process Science Center (PSL), San Francisco, California, USA

Landscape architect: MPA Design. Project team: Michael Painter, David W. Nelson. Client: Genentech Corporation administered by Flad and Associates. General contractor: Rudolph & Sletten Inc. Landscape contractor: B & B Landscaping Inc. Building architect: Flad and Associates. Irrigation consultant: Russell D. Mitchell and Associates. Electrical consultant: Affiliated Engineers Inc. Civil engineer: Brian Kangas Foulk. Pavers: Hanover Architectural Products. Slate paving: Vermont Structural Slate Company. Benches, chairs and tables: Forms and Surfaces. Irrigation equipment: Rainbird.

Photographic Credits

The author and the publisher would like to thank all the designers and architects who submitted work for inclusion in this book and the photographers whose work is reproduced. The following photographic credits are given, with page numbers in brackets: Henré Abbadie (150-1, 156-7); Aero Camera Hofmeester (80 bottom); Matthew Andrews (90, 98, 99 top); Courtesy Aspinwall Clouston (118-19); Poul Buchard (38, 40-1); Courtesy Camlin Lonsdale (86, 89); Dixi Carillo (30-1, 159 bottom, 160-1); S. Crockett (142-3); Marsh Davis (37 top right); Courtesy Michiel den Ruijter (80 top); G. Dufresne (130); Alan Eachus (32-3 top); Strode Eckert (114-15 top); Courtesy Environmental Design Partnership (108-11); Gabriel Figueroa Flores (94-7); Jens Frederiksen (43); Mistumasa Fujitsuka (50-1); Courtesy Eric Fulford (37 left); Jeff Goldberg/ESTO (138-41); Courtesy K. Gustafson (58-59, 60 bottom, 61, 176-7); Manfred Hanisch (144-7, 152, 170-5); Courtesy Hanna/Olin (64-5); Hargreaves Associates (28-9, 154-5); George Heinrich (56-7); Haruo Hirota (66, 68-9, 166-9); Robert Holden (18-21, 33 bottom, 78, 81); Martin Jones (116-17); Douglas Kahn (178, 179 bottom); Tom Lamb (104-7); Courtesy Ricardo Legorreta (123-5); Jannes Linders (148, 149 centre); Courtesy Louisiana Museum (42); Ben Luxmore (44-7); Phillipe Marchand (60 top); Courtesy MBM Arquitectes (75, 77); Mistuo Mastuoka (112-13 top); Ian Menzies (100-2, 103 bottom); Wayne Miles (103); Satoru Misima – Nikkei BPCo (113 bottom); Monika Nikolic (9, 12-17, 22-7); Tom Noz (52-4); Luis On (70, 72-4, 82-5); Michael Painter (179 top, 180, 182, 184-5); Pamela Palmer (158, 159 top, 162-5); Michael Parker (115 bottom); Georg Penker (62-3); Erhard Pfeiffer (122); Arne Saelen (128-9); Graham Sands (99 bottom); Eric Schleef – illustrator (36); Hiroshi Shinozawa (136-7); Shodo Suzuki (126-7); Hidenori Takei (120, 132-5); Jay Venezia Photography (34-5); G. Vexlard (131); Courtesy West 8 (92-3, 149 top and bottom); Courtesy Robin Winogrond (48-9).

Index of Designers & Projects